Finding Your Voice in Law School

Finding Your Voice in Law School

*Mastering Classroom Cold Calls, Job Interviews,
and Other Verbal Challenges*

Molly Bishop Shadel

CAROLINA ACADEMIC PRESS
Durham, North Carolina

Library of Congress Cataloging-in-Publication Data

Shadel, Molly Bishop, 1969–
  Finding your voice in law school : mastering classroom cold calls, job inter-
views, and other verbal challenges / Molly Bishop Shadel.
    pages. cm
  Includes bibliographical references and index.
  ISBN 978-1-61163-073-2
1. Law students--United States--Handbooks, manuals, etc. 2. Law--Study
and teaching--United States. 3. Law--Vocational guidance--United States. I.
Title.
  KF283.S583 2012
  340.071'173--dc23   2012037605

Carolina Academic Press
700 Kent Street
Durham, NC 27701
Telephone (919) 489-7486
Fax (919) 493-5668
www.cap-press.com

Printed in the United States of America

Contents

Acknowledgments   ix

Prologue   xi

**Chapter One · The Socratic Method: Learning to Think
Like a Lawyer**   3

Where Did the Socratic Method Come From?   8

Why Should You Try to Master the Socratic Method?   9

Chapter Two · The Socratic Method: How to Prepare for Class   13

Strategy One: Devise a Plan to Keep Up with the Reading   14

Strategy Two: Read for Particular Things   17

What Is the Law, Anyway?   18

Pay Attention to Precedent   19

The Text Matters   20

The Importance of Authority   21

Using Analogy Well   22

Avoid Logical Fallacies   22

Strategy Three: Tactical Note-Taking, the One-Page Brief, and
Course Outlines   24

Chapter Three · The Socratic Method: Strategies in the Classroom   31

Strategy One: Pay Attention in Class   31

Strategy Two: Techniques for Answering the Question   32

Strategy Three: What to Do If You Don't Know the Answer   37

Strategy Four: Learn to Overcome Self-Consciousness   41

Strategy Five: Predict the Questions   43

Chapter Four · Making a Formal Presentation in a Class or on the Job   51

Your Goals: Ethos, Pathos and Logos   52

Writing the Presentation 53
    Find a Theme 53
    Craft Your Structure 54
    Pay Special Attention to Your First and Last Paragraphs 55
    Get Their Attention Back 56
    Use Clear Language 56
Give Yourself Ample Rehearsal Time 57
Speaking on Short Notice 58
Delivery Matters 59
    What to Do with Your Feet 60
    What to Do with Your Hands 62
    Use Your Best Voice 63
    Make Eye Contact 65
    Think About Rhythm: Pausing and Pace 66
Overcoming Fear of Public Speaking 67
Final Thoughts 69

Chapter Five · First-Year Moot Court and Beyond 71
What Is an Oral Argument? 71
Before the Oral Argument 72
    How to Prepare 72
    The Importance of Practicing 74
At the Oral Argument 75
    What to Expect on the Big Day 75
    What to Bring to the Lectern 75
    Beginning the Argument 76
    Answering Questions During Argument 77
    Using the Right Language 79
    Striking the Right Tone 80

Chapter Six · Trial Practice Classes and Mock Trial Teams 83
What a Trial Looks Like 84
The Importance of Credibility (*Ethos*) 86
Engage the Jury's Attention (*Pathos*) 88
Persuade Them with Logic (*Logos*) 89
The Opening Statement 90
Direct Examination 93
    Refreshing a Witness's Recollection 96
    Entering an Exhibit into Evidence 96
Cross-Examination 98

Impeaching a Witness   99
Arguing Objections   101
Closing Argument   102

Chapter Seven · Leading a Student Organization   107
The Benefits of Leadership Experience   107
How to Lead a Meeting   108
Prepare an Agenda in Advance   109
Respect People's Time   109
Consider What Should Be Accomplished Outside of a Meeting 110
Keep the Meeting Productive and the Conversation on Track 111
Set the Right Tone   113
Delegate Tasks Effectively   114
Expect the Unexpected   114

Chapter Eight · Interacting with Professors   117
Interactions in the Classroom   117
Interactions Outside of the Classroom   119
Electronic Communications   119
Meeting with Professors   120
Working for Professors   121
Securing Letters of Recommendation   122

Chapter Nine · Job Interviews   125
First-Round and Callback Interviews: The Basic Structure   125
Preparing for the Interview   126
Know Your Resume   126
Find Your Theme   127
Know Why You Want This Job   127
Deal with Bad Facts Gracefully   128
Know the Employer   130
Know Your Classes   130
Know About the World   130
Know the Answers to Basic Interview Questions   130
Practice for the Interview   131
Vocal Tips   131
Mastering Nonverbal Communication   132
What to Wear   133
During the Interview   136
Special Issues for Callback Interviews   137
How to Network   139

Chapter Ten · Communicating on the Job   141
  Electronic Communications   142
  In-Person Meetings   143
  Asking Questions   144
  Professional Behavior   145
    Dress Professionally   146
    Turn in Your Assignments on Time   146
    Show Up to Work on Time and Work for the Entire Workday   146
    Take Any Legal Training Classes the Employer Offers   146
    Beware of Multitasking   147
    Social Events   147

Epilogue   151

Appendix of Cases and Rules   153
  Vokes v. Arthur Murray, Inc.   153
  Lucy v. Zehmer   158
  Regina v. Faulkner   166
  Hilder v. St. Peter   171
  Selected Federal Rules of Evidence   180

Index   185

Acknowledgments

I am very grateful to the students (some of whom were also my research assistants), faculty, and members of the legal profession who graciously shared their thoughts with me in preparation for this book. They are: Kerry Abrams, Karin Agness, Charles Barzun, Natalie Brown, Tomiko Brown-Nagin, Jon Cannon, C. Benjamin Cooper, Alexander Creticos, Katherine Mims Crocker, Tore deBella, Virginia Davis, David Demirbilek, Holly Duke, Lydie Essama, Kim Forde-Mazrui, Joe Fore, Jenna Gallagher, Rebecca Gantt, Brandon Garrett, George Geis, Jeree Harris, Toby Heytens, Demetria Johnson, Nate Kenser, David Leahy, Ben Martin, Timothy McKernan, Brian Mink, Daniel Nicolich, Andrew Peach, Kent Piacenti, Caitlin McLaughlin Poe, Gage Raley, George Rutherglen, Bob Sayler, Kristen Shepherd, Henry Sire, Chris Sprigman, Cory Stott, Steven Sun, Holly Vrandenburgh, Daniel Watkins, and Ann Woolhandler. I owe a special debt of thanks to Mary Wood, whose editing skills are superb, and to Troy Dunaway and the University of Virginia School of Law, for setting up the research and editing support that I needed. Finally, thanks to my family for making work-life balance possible.

Prologue

On my first day of law school, I was terrified. I had the sense that my class-mates had always known that they wanted to be lawyers, and probably had majored in some sort of "pre-law" subject in college. They already knew a lot about the legal system, I imagined, from some college class they had taken (and I had missed). They probably spent their summers working at law firms, read all the newspapers and books that lawyers read, and mastered the basics that I should have already acquired somewhere along the way, but hadn't. When I started law school, I felt like some weird interloper in a world that wasn't mine.

To prepare for my first class, I completed the assigned reading and I also watched *The Paper Chase*. Doing the reading was a good idea. Watching the movie wasn't. *The Paper Chase* is a fictionalized account about how humiliating law school can seem, and I became petrified about "The Socratic Method." As the movie portrayed the method, a professor calls on a student in front of a huge classroom full of people and asks questions that no one could possibly answer. It seemed to me that the whole point of the Socratic Method was to showcase the student's ignorance, not so anyone would learn from it, but so people would laugh.

My most terrifying nightmare came true the next day. I walked into my first class—Legal Methods—sat down, and opened my book. The professor looked up and said, "Ms. Bishop?" And so it began.

I have no idea what question I was asked or what I said because the whole experience seemed so traumatic. But I can remember my next cold call, because it happened during the first meeting of my next class. The scene: Contracts. The first student called on? Me. And then again in Civil Procedure (where I was called on every week for the rest of the semester). The professor quizzed me in my first Copyright Law class as well, and also in Corporations, where, as in Civ Pro, I was one of the stable of students called on again and again and again.

I am now a law school professor, and I have a theory about why I so often was called on first. It wasn't because anyone was out to get me—it was because my last name ("Bishop") was near the beginning of the alphabet and was easy to pronounce. I think professors continued to call on me because I hadn't mastered legal jargon, so when I answered their questions, I used words that everyone in the room could understand. Also, I didn't break down under questioning (much as I might have wanted to). Most importantly, I quickly developed strategies to make it through class without making a fool of myself. I was not very good at the Socratic Method when I started law school, but by the time I graduated, I was an expert.

Performing well in class didn't always guarantee me a good grade. I was surprised to discover that the same professor who called on me week after week had no qualms about giving me an unspectacular grade, because for many classes only the final exam counts. But even if it didn't always help my transcript, I now think that the verbal education I received in law school was more important than any grade. Being able to articulate an idea aloud, to think under pressure, to keep your cool in a stressful situation—these are the skills that can make you stand out a job interview. Once you have the job, your skills of verbal persuasion can help you succeed in it. I found that when I joined a law firm, I could snag more interesting assignments simply because I was willing to speak up at team meetings and could articulate my ideas effectively. I served my clients better because I could communicate effectively with and for them. Now that I'm a law school professor, I draw on my rhetorical education every day to teach classes and make presentations. It is worth the time to learn how to speak effectively, because it's a skill you will use for the rest of your life.

The good news is that anyone can learn to speak well. *Anyone*. As a professor who teaches oral advocacy and rhetoric, I have seen student after student face the challenge of public speaking. I've seen them overcome their fears, stumble, get back up again, practice, and improve. Yes, there are some people who are naturals at this. But anyone can become competent, even brilliant, at verbal persuasion. The purpose of this book is to help you figure out how.

Finding Your Voice
in Law School

Chapter One

The Socratic Method: Learning to Think Like a Lawyer

One of the more memorable rites of passage for many aspiring lawyers is learning to cope with the Socratic Method in law school.

The Socratic Method is a particular way of teaching that you may not have encountered in high school or college. It usually looks something like this. You and approximately 80 of your classmates are seated in a large classroom. The professor stands at the lectern at the front of the room. To prepare for class, you have read several *cases* (judicial opinions). Perhaps you have also read a statute or regulation, or a contract.

The professor selects a student (often at random) and begins to quiz him or her about one of the cases. The questions are rarely limited to requiring the student to recite the facts of the case. Instead, the student might be asked to explain why the case was decided in the way it was, what the ramifications of the case are, what might happen if some fact of the case were changed, how the logic of the judge's decision worked, how the case is similar to or different from other cases that the class is studying, and so forth. Here is what a (fictional) contracts class using the Socratic Method might sound like:

Professor: So let's turn to *Vokes v. Arthur Murray.*[1] Ms. Smith, what is going on in this case?

Student: Okay. The defendant, Arthur Murray, owned a dance school, and Ms. Vokes was this 51-year-old widow who wanted to find a "new interest" in life. She bought dance classes and paid for them in advance.

Student quotes from opinion — a good practice because often the exact wording is mportant.

---

1. 212 So.2d 906 (Fla. Dist. Ct. App. 1968). The case is reprinted in the Appendix.

Then later, she sued to have the money for the classes refunded because she said they lied to her about her dance skills.

Professor: Well, did the folks at Arthur Murray lie to her?

Student: The case says that they praised her grace and poise, and that Murray painted a picture that she was "an excellent dancer."

Professor: And what did Vokes have to say about that?

Student: Vokes argued that this wasn't true. The case said she lacked the ability to "hear the musical beat." And that while she first thought that she was in the "spring of her life," or something like that, that there was really "no spring in her life or her feet." [The class laughs.]

Again, the student is using good technique by quoting from the opinion. You are more likely to be accurate if you quote rather than paraphrase.

Professor: Could this just be a case of buyer's regret?

Student: Well, I'm pretty sure she was a bad dancer.

Professor: Could it be that at that early point in her illustrious, but eventually doomed, dancing career when the lessons were sold to her, she did have the grace and poise suggestive of "an excellent dancer"?

Student: [Slightly confused] Um, I mean, she was old. [Laughter.] I mean, I don't think someone can have a bunch of potential one year, and then the next just be terrible.

Professor: Well, how do we know she's a bad dancer now?

This is a better way to answer the question than the way the student answered the first time. Rather than just guessing that she was a bad dancer because of her age, look for evidence of it in the text of the case.

Student: I guess because she said she is. And also, I guess the complaint stated that the employees at Arthur Murray knew that she was. They knew she had no "dance aptitude" and they sold her $30,000 in dance lessons anyway.

Professor: That's certainly a lot of dance lessons. [Laughter.] But what if that many lessons are required to become a great dancer? Maybe she needed initial encouragement at first, and $30,000 later, she would become great. After so many dance lessons, she's bound to get better, right?

Student: [Still slightly confused with the line of questioning.] I ... I guess so?

Professor: Even ignoring whether she was becoming a great dancer, do you think that Ms. Vokes was gaining a benefit from the transaction?

Student: Well, probably. I mean she got to go to all these dance lessons. They probably at least entertained her, and maybe she benefited from having her ego stroked like that.

Professor: So then, should she be allowed to rescind the contract? And if you think so, on what theory?

Student: [More confused.] I guess she shouldn't?

Professor: Well, what theory for rescission is asserted in the case?

Student: The case says that she is trying to rescind based on fraud because Arthur Murray knew she had no dance skills, and that she was not developing properly. It says they kept lying to her, telling her that she had "grace and poise" and whatnot, when they knew that she did not. And the reason they were doing this was to sell her more dance lessons.

Professor: And what does Arthur Murray argue?

Student: I think ... I think ... they argue that their statements were opinions and not fact.

Professor: Does that matter?

Student: [More confidently.] Yeah, it does. The *Restatement of Contracts*[2] says that fraud requires misrepresentation of a fact, that the fact misrepresented be "material," and that the person misled justifiably relied upon the misrepresentation.

Professor: So can someone be a bad dancer ... in fact?

Student: Yeaaa ... I mean ... I guess ... No. I mean ... I guess a lot of people could agree that you are

This would be a stronger answer if the student would take a position and defend it, rather than offering the answer as a question. Most every case you encounter in law school can be argued both ways, so choose a side and try to defend it with conviction. If you practice sounding confident, you will become more confident. This is also a question the student could have anticipated and should have been prepared to address.

The professor is throwing the student a lifeline here. If the student can articulate the position that the court took, then the student can either agree with it or disagree with it. The professor is hinting at how the student might go about formulating an answer.

This is a good answer. The student has just hit upon a very important issue raised by the case—whether the statements were fact or opinion—and is offering a test from a persuasive source that could resolve the issue.

This answer would be better without the filler sounds. Take a moment to think, and then answer, rather than stalling with verbal garbage. A pause is preferable to filler noises.

---

2. *The Restatement of Contracts* is a legal treatise that summarizes and clarifies the basic principles of contract law that have been adopted in various jurisdictions.

bad, but I guess I don't see how it can be an absolute fact. It would have to be an opinion.

Professor: So if we are not dealing with a misrepresentation of a fact, then what theory does the court use to allow the complaint?

Student: The court says when there is a special relationship, and one party has superior knowledge, that that party's false opinions can be fraudulent. And that the Arthur Murray people did not speak the "whole truth" because if they had, Vokes wouldn't have bought all those lessons.

Bingo. She's getting this right.

Professor: It seems the court is desperate to find a theory to let this case proceed. This is actually the fourth time Vokes amended her complaint. They finally allow it based on this special relationship theory. But why should this be a special relationship? Is Murray a fiduciary? Does the company have any responsibility to make sure that Vokes is apprised of the entire truth?

This is an important concept and a way to disagree with what the court said. The student is doing well at this point.

Student: No. They are two parties at arms-length.

Professor: So do we want courts finding "special relationships" with two parties at arms-length? How do we know when one party can justifiably be said to have "superior knowledge"?

This is the answer that the professor is looking for. The student has now taken a position — contrary to the position that the court took — and is defending it.

Student: [Trying to follow the leading questions.] I guess it makes things much more confusing. It opens the door for people to assert that the other party had "superior knowledge" and thus should reveal all their information to the other party in pretty much any case where you are selling something.

Professor: Here's a hypothetical. Say I am a used-car dealer, and you are looking to purchase a used car. I have been in the business for the past 20 years of my life, and I think that this particular car is worth between $5,000 and $8,000 dollars. But being a used-car salesman, I list the car with a sticker of $10,000. You come along and tell me that you don't know much about cars, but you desperately need a car today and you like this particular one. I tell you all this great stuff about the car, but it's clear puffery—general opinions—"A real beauty ... You won't be disappointed"—and whatnot. You purchase the car for $10,000. Later, you say you relied on my opinions and bought a car that you otherwise would not have bought. Can you rescind later based on this "superior knowledge" theory?

Student: Well, that seems like a problem. It would require parties to always reveal their bargaining information, and would severely restrict sales tactics, and would allow for people to easily go back on their contracts. So, I want to say no. You should not be able to rescind.

Professor: What about for rowing lessons on a river, after I tell you that you look like you can become an Olympic rower, when I think you have no chance? Is this just sales puffery, or is it fraud? What if I know you are taking my appraisal very seriously in your decision?

Student: I guess that fact pattern is closer to the facts of the *Arthur Murray* case, but it also raises a policy problem. It opens the door for people to easily rescind contracts, when we don't know if they relied on the opinions in the first place and we don't know what other benefits from the activity they were receiving. At the same time, if you're talking to an expert, you want to be able to trust that you can rely on his opinion.

The student has done well. She has applied the lessons learned from the original case to new fact patterns.

Professor: I agree. However, the *Arthur Murray* case opens the door to a lot of potential line-drawing problems. If the court is going to allow the case to proceed, I think it would be best that they refine the theory on which they base their decision. As it stands, it is a very muddy opinion to work with. And so ... that's all the time we have for today.

You can see how intimidating it might be for a student to answer questions like the ones in the discussion above, but you can also see that the student's understanding of the case is much deeper at the end of the conversation than it was at the beginning. She is able to articulate a distinction between fact and opinion in fraud cases, and she sees the problems with the "special relationship" theory upon which the court ultimately relies. By the end of the discussion, she has correctly identified the important factual issues in the case, the theory upon which the court reaches its decision, and the potential ramifications of the decision for future lawsuits. Most importantly, she started to gain confidence in her ability to analyze a legal issue and explain it to someone else.

In the hands of a skilled professor, the Socratic Method encourages law students to look beyond their own idiosyncratic reactions to a particular case to see how it fits into the broader fabric of the law, how the underlying principles of a case can be used as tools to help the lawyer represent clients in other cases, and how the framing of a dispute can sometimes lead to dramatically different outcomes. It also teaches law students to think under pressure and to articulate those ideas aloud, and to take and defend a position — in other words, to think like a lawyer.

Where Did the Socratic Method Come From?

Based on a mode of teaching similar to one used by Socrates in ancient Greece, the Socratic Method was introduced to law schools in 1870 and almost immediately began to transform how law was taught. Until that point, American law schools were fairly informal. Law students attended lectures — if they chose to — and self-reported their accomplishments (rather than being graded by a professor) on their way to a diploma one or two years later. There were no academic prerequisites for admission to law school, no required courses, and no exams. It sounds less stressful than law school today, perhaps, but the system also did not ensure that graduates had actually learned anything about the law.

In 1870, Christopher Columbus Langdell became dean of Harvard Law School. That same year, he published *Selection of Cases on the Law of Contracts*, a textbook in which he described law as "a science." The best way to master that science, he said, was "by studying the cases in which it is embodied." In his classes, Dean Langdell began methodically questioning his students in class about the cases in the textbook, seeking to provoke active, critical thinking in order to reconstruct the underlying doctrines. Soon, law schools all over the country were using Langdell's method.[3]

---

3. You can read about the history of the Socratic Method in William M. Sullivan *et al*, *Educating Lawyers: Preparation for the Profession of Law* (2007) and in Peggy C. Davis & Elizabeth E. Steinglass, *A Dialogue About Socratic Teaching*, 23 *NYU Rev. L. & Soc. Change* 249, 261–264 (1997).

While the Socratic Method is no longer the exclusive teaching method used in law schools, it remains the most recognizable one, and most professors will undoubtedly use some form of it, particularly in first-year classes. It allows a single professor to teach large groups of students while providing those students with some opportunity to practice their verbal skills—a cost-effective model for a law school.

Why Should You Try to Master the Socratic Method?

Many law students are motivated to figure out how to do well when called upon in class simply to avoid looking or feeling foolish in front of their peers. However, you may have read law school prep books that advise that the only thing that really matters in law school is grades, which often depend entirely on how well you do on the single, written exam given at the end of most classes. So, naturally, you might be tempted to spend all your time preparing for that exam rather than honing your speaking skills.

But the Socratic Method is meant to give you a chance to practice the kind of thinking required to succeed on an exam. When you take a law school exam, you must do more than simply state the facts of every case that you have encountered, or name all the legal principles that are central to the area of law in question. You must *apply* those legal principles to the fact pattern posed by the exam, and *analogize* or *distinguish* the fact patterns of other cases from the facts of yours. There will be very few facts for you to memorize before you come into a law school exam—the date of a particular judicial opinion, for example, is unlikely to score you any points. Instead, the professor will be testing your deeper understanding of why the law is the way it is, and how the different components of it can work together to result in a particular outcome. When you listen to the Socratic questioning going on in your classes, you are being offered an inside view into the sorts of questions a good lawyer might ask himself when confronted with a legal issue. Pay attention to the questions and the answers your classmates give, and think about how you might answer the same questions. The Socratic Method is not something to block out or survive—it is a way to practice, day after day, the sort of thinking that will help you score well on an exam, and later, the sort of thinking critical to being a lawyer.

Once you leave law school and begin legal practice, you may be surprised to find that your verbal skills become far more important than what appears on your transcript. Here is an account from one lawyer who graduated from Columbia Law School, where she performed well enough to join the Law Review. She then went to a leading law firm, and had the following experience:

> I remember being astonished during my first several months at a law firm that no one cared that I'd made better grades in law school than one of my classmates who started at the firm with me. She'd done well enough to get a job at the firm, but she hadn't made Law Review or clerked like I had. She hadn't gotten an 'A' in Contracts, like I had. Nonetheless, she was the star of the practice group to which we were both assigned. She had made enough genuine connections during her time as a summer associate at the firm that she'd felt comfortable inviting law firm partners to her wedding, and they had all come. She was very good at speaking up in team meetings, while I felt too unsure of myself to say a word. She used firm social functions as an opportunity to continue to hone connections that got her great assignments. She ultimately made partner at that firm.

The lawyer telling this tale realized she needed to make a change to excel at her job.

> I decided that I should follow her example of becoming a more visible member of the team. After all, I had figured out how to handle cold calls, and this required precisely the same skill set—speaking under pressure. So any time the firm needed someone to make a presentation at a practice group lunch or sit on a summer associate panel, I raised my hand (just as I had done as a defensive measure in some of my more intimidating classes). Any time there was a trial practice training program that would give me the chance to make an opening statement or a closing argument before my colleagues, I signed up. I started to think of firm social events as part of the job, and I assigned myself the task of striking up a conversation with at least one new person at each event. I made myself say something at every team meeting. I wasn't working the longest hours of my fellow associates, but partners noticed me and had a favorable impression of my abilities. The result—I, too, started to earn plum assignments. It's not enough to sit around and think deep thoughts. You have to share them with other people, and the most direct way to do that is to speak up.

Good grades help you get a job interview, but verbal presentation skills are required to actually land the job and succeed in it. (See Chapter Nine for help with succeeding in a job interview.) In today's economy, you cannot simply say, "I have a law degree. I have good grades; now hire and promote me." You have to find a way to shine and add value. Being able to articulate an idea aloud helps show those around you that you are smart and talented, and because it will make you a better advocate, it benefits your colleagues and your clients as well.

The Socratic classroom provides a great opportunity for you to practice these skills. If you can figure out how to manage the Socratic Method, you will acquire abilities that you will draw on frequently in your legal practice. You will find that you can speak up even if the environment is intimidating, making you more likely to express your ideas aloud during team meetings at law firms or when challenged in court. Participating in class over time will help you become more articulate, which helps you learn how to express your thoughts artfully, and you will also find that nothing truly terrible happens if someone disagrees with you. In fact, if you stick to your guns and present a good argument, you'll see that can persuade people to accept your point of view—a useful skill for a lawyer indeed.

So how should you get ready to shine in the Socratic classroom? Chapter Two will show you how to prepare for class, and Chapter Three will help you do well once you are there. Other chapters in the book will explore the many ways that improving your verbal presentation skills can help you in law school, your career, and beyond.

Chapter Two

The Socratic Method: How to Prepare for Class

What strategies can you use to succeed in a class that uses the Socratic Method? This chapter will offer you ideas about what to do as you read for class, while Chapter Three will discuss techniques to use during the class itself.

To prepare these chapters, I asked fellow faculty members at the University of Virginia School of Law to supply me with the names of students who were particularly skilled at handling the Socratic Method. I made an effort to approach professors across a wide range of subjects, and tried to include people from different backgrounds (in terms of gender, race, ethnicity, and political stripes). The students they identified proved to be as varied as the faculty that I approached. They came from a range of backgrounds (socio-economically and geographically), ages (ranging from early 20s to mid-40s), and races (Caucasian, African-American, Asian, and Latino). They were roughly equal in terms of gender. I interviewed as many of these students as I could in an effort to learn why they were able to outshine their classmates.

Interestingly, student after student expressed surprise to hear that he or she had been identified by a faculty member as being effective in class. I note this because it indicates to me, first, that professors are not always clear about signaling when you are doing well in class, so don't take this lack of praise as a sign that you have not performed well; and second, that the professors were not impressed by know-it-alls. Every student who met with me was disarmingly nice, and I suspect that tone had something to do with the favorable impressions they made. (I'll say more about tone in the next chapter.) Also, it could be that most everyone feels insecure about public speaking and evaluates their performance more harshly than others do.

There is no single "right" way to approach speaking well in a law school class, as you will see through some of the many experiences of the surveyed students.

But several common strategies for success did emerge during the course of these interviews.

Strategy One: Devise a Plan to Keep Up with the Reading

Tim had just finished his second year of law school when he met with me to talk about his experiences in class. The professor who identified Tim is one of the best on our faculty at teaching and leading classroom discussions. The professor also possesses substantial real-world business experience that has made him particularly good at communicating and thinking on his feet. If this professor recognized these same qualities in Tim, then Tim was someone I wanted to meet.

But Tim appeared shocked that he had been singled out for doing well in class, because apparently these abilities had not translated into particularly strong grades. Tim told me:

> First year was really tough for me. Never in my life had I really been expected to actually recall all that I've learned over a semester for a single exam. It didn't even occur to me to the end when I was trying to prepare for the exam that I would need to see a big picture. I was not putting things together at all.
>
> I was so disappointed first semester with my grades.... When it came to studying for finals, I was just really paralyzed because I didn't even know where to start.

The experience of feeling lost during the first semester of law school is common. Many of us come from colleges where the professor tells us (via lecturing) what we need to learn, and tests our learning periodically through papers, a midterm, and a final exam. By contrast, classes in law school rarely consist of teaching to memorize texts and facts. Law is fluid. When you become a lawyer, you are rarely able to tell a client, "Ah, I have looked it up, and the law clearly says ____." Being a lawyer means taking something that sounds concrete, like a statute or regulation, and then looking at it from all angles to figure out how it applies to your client's situation.

That means you will not be reading a textbook that tells you in a succinct paragraph or two, "Property law works like this." Instead, it means that in most classes, you will be reading some statutes and many published opinions in which you see the law being developed through the facts of particular cases. You will read scores of these cases because the law changes, and understanding how one case builds on another gives you a fuller understanding of the law.

In many classes, that reading load will be quite heavy because it requires a different kind of reading than what you might have practiced in college. It's not enough to simply read the cases. You have to read them and then think about them. You have to understand what happened (the facts of the case, the parties involved, and so forth), what the court said, why the court said it, and whether it was the right thing to say. You have to be able to unpack the court's reasoning so that you can apply it to a future case. You have to be able to explain whether you agree with the decision, and why (or why not). And you need to see where the individual case fits into the bigger picture of what you are learning in that class, and why. So you need to give yourself time not just to read, but also to take notes and think.

If you haven't been able to keep up with the reading, you will find yourself struggling as the semester wears on. Tim had this experience:

> I got cold-called in Civ Pro the first day and it was pretty clear he was going down the list, so Civ Pro became a big casualty of my [lax] reading since I wasn't going to be called on again. I always intended to read the cases later, but instead I ended up with a kind of kamikaze approach, which is just out of control and scrambling. It sometimes would leave me up until 3 a.m. That's just not really sustainable. It was just impossible to get everything done.

The stress in his voice as he described his first semester was palpable.

I asked Tim why he thinks that he did well in his Corporations class, but not in some of his other courses. He explained that his Corporations professor usually assigned a reasonable amount of reading, so he was able to read it all and take the time to digest it. In classes with more challenging workloads, he was not able to take this time and as a result did not do as well. Tim's experience illustrates one of the first truisms of law school: *You cannot succeed if you haven't done the reading*. This theme surfaced again and again in my interviews with students—the stars always did the reading, no matter what. Nothing can substitute for good preparation, and little can save you if you are unprepared. In the class in which he kept up with the reading load, Tim was a star. In others, he felt like a failure.

Tim is admirable because he thought strategically about his situation and took steps to change it. This is another important thing to recognize—law school does not come easily to most people at first, but you have control over this. You can change the outcome if you examine and change the behaviors that aren't helping you.

Tim's solution was to treat law school like a job. "Get there in the morning, stay until you're done," he said. If he thinks he is going to be on call, he reads through the opinions twice, the second time during the 24 hours before class so that the case will be fresh in his mind. He arms himself with notes in the margins: "If it's the holding, I'll write in block letters 'HOLDING'; if there are three prongs to the test I'll write, 'Prong Number 1.'" He is also careful to read the whole paragraph first before writing anything, "because I find that you can sort of become a zombie underlining, and not actually read."

The workload in law school can be quite difficult, and you must develop a strategy to handle it. This usually includes devising a daily schedule with time set aside for reading, attending classes, exercising, socializing, and sleeping. Realistically, you are going to need to work a 9- to 11-hour day most of the time you are in school, which includes preparing for and attending classes. You can have a lighter schedule on the weekends, but you should plan to work on the weekends as well or you won't get it all done. These are the same hours that you are likely to find yourself working as an attorney, especially when you are just starting out.

Exercise and socializing are necessary to keep sane, so include them in your schedule, but they *must* take a back seat to studying. It will not last forever, but during your first year, consider adjusting your life so that you can log long hours studying in the library. Warn your family and friends so they will support your need for solitude. Your fellow classmates can be encouraging during this time because they are going through the same experience.

Figure out the times of day your mind is the most fresh, and read during those times. If you regularly doze off when you read after lunch, then don't read after lunch — try studying early in the morning instead, or in the mid-afternoon after you've gotten some exercise. Schedule yourself some time every day to flip back through what you've highlighted in your reading to get the "big picture." Often, it's smart to do this at the end of the day — use the last 15 minutes of your study time to figure out how what you've read that day fits into what you've already learned and where the course is going. A law school workload can seem daunting, but you can handle it if you chip away at it regularly, every single day. Don't try to cram it all in at the end. If you do, it will overwhelm you.

Developing good, disciplined study habits during law school teaches you two skills that are critical to good lawyering — diligence and time management. Lawyers often face a mountain of work, particularly at times of crisis for their clients. A good lawyer tackles that mountain head-on and masters it. You cannot do this if you squander your time "getting ready" to work, or if you work inefficiently, for example by reading something but not actually absorbing any of it, or stopping mid-paragraph to surf the Internet or watch TV. To show you have mastered a semester's worth of material on a single exam, you will have to develop the self-discipline to work on a subject each day. You have to set internal deadlines for yourself to do well. If you learn how to do this now, while you are in law school, you'll find that you are better able to succeed at your law practice in the future.

Tim understandably was frustrated by the fact that speaking well in class did not translate into good grades in all his classes. But that doesn't mean he won't be an excellent lawyer. In fact, Tim may end up being a better lawyer than his classmates who perform well on exams but who cannot speak well publicly, because he finds it easier to convey his ideas. Law school exams don't usually test verbal skills because an oral exam would be prohibitively time-consuming in a large class managed by a single professor. Nor are written exams perfect proxies for how good a lawyer a student is likely to become. So it's not uncommon for a student who has done extremely well on exams to struggle with advocating a position or counseling a client in practice. But Tim can articulate his ideas, and that will be invaluable to him in his career.

Also, by speaking aloud in class, Tim made himself stand out in the eyes of his professor. That professor will be able to write a more persuasive recommendation letter for Tim, whom he knows in a more personal way because of their in-class exchanges, than he could for the student who may have aced his exam but who never spoke up in class. (See Chapter Eight, on interacting with professors, for a longer discussion of this topic.)

Strategy Two: Read for Particular Things

As you read the material for the day, prepare strategically for being called on in class. This involves giving yourself time to process what you have read and arming yourself with written notes that will help you during a cold call.

During your first semester of law school, whether or not you know you will be called on, take the time to read through the material twice. Minimize distractions as you read—turn off the music or the TV. The first time, read for comprehension. If you don't understand something, read it again. The second time, think about how what you've read fits into the bigger picture of what you are learning. As you move forward in your legal studies, you will find that it becomes easier to read cases, and you may not have to re-read the material as often. Your note-taking abilities will improve as well. But when you are starting out, and any time you know that you're on call, reading the material twice will build your knowledge of how to read law and prepare to discuss it in class.

The first time you read a legal opinion, you may feel overwhelmed by the amount of information the opinion contains. It can be difficult at first blush to discern what's significant and what you can gloss over. You will get better at this over time, simply through experience, but the following is a quick primer on what is likely to be important in the material.

What Is the Law, Anyway?

America is a *common law* system, which means that we do not rely exclusively on laws written down in books (as a *civil law* system would).[1] We have codified laws (*statutes*), and they are important, but equally important is what judges have said about those laws in judicial opinions. These judicial opinions are the cases you'll spend most of your time reading in law school, and the *holding* (the decision) in each opinion is as much the law as any statute is. The law also comes from *constitutions* (both federal and state), *treaties*, and *regulations* (rules made by an agency at either the state or federal level pursuant to a statute). You might be reading any of these sources for class, but you will spend the bulk of your time reading judicial opinions.

The reason you don't simply memorize statutes in law school is because the law changes as the needs of society change. The statute you might memorize today might not be the same statute that will be on the books when you are practicing law. By focusing instead on judicial opinions, you can understand why the judges made the decisions that they made. If you can begin to "think like a lawyer" yourself, then you'll know what arguments will best persuade a judge on behalf of your client. What the judge says becomes part of the law, and you can influence it with your argument.

The judicial opinions you will read in law school involve the most complicated legal questions. In these cases, both sides of the dispute thought they stood a good chance of winning. The cases even made it to the Supreme Court, which means that reasonable minds disagreed about the outcome, and were able to articulate arguments persuasive enough to make it through several layers of judicial review. In actual legal practice, the vast majority of cases will have

---

1. As some point in your legal career, you may learn about the laws of other countries, such as those in continental Europe. These legal systems are called *civil law* systems, in which the law is contained in written-down rules, called *codes*. Judges in these systems interpret the code and make sure it is followed, but they are not bound by earlier decisions of judges. The U.S. legal system, in contrast, is a *common law* system, which means that our law is derived primarily from judges deciding particular disputes and writing about them. What the judges say about the law is every bit as important — in some instances, more important — than the language of the law itself. For a helpful discussion of this topic, and of legal reasoning in general, *see* Frederick Schauer, *Thinking Like a Lawyer: A New Introduction to Legal Reasoning* 104–107 (2009).

clearer outcomes than those you study in school, but we use the hard ones in law school to help you learn.

Pay Attention to Precedent

Legal analysis is a special way of thinking. In a quarrel with your parents, you are unlikely to be persuaded by their argument that you should do something because "that's the way it's always been done." When you become a lawyer, however, you realize that if you're advocating a position that has never been taken before, and no judicial opinions support what you're trying to do, then likely you will be on the losing side of the argument. *Precedent* is extremely important in the law.

Precedent means following the decisions that have been handed down in the past, either by a higher court, such as the Supreme Court or the Court of Appeals in your jurisdiction (*vertical precedent*), or by the court before which you are appearing (*horizontal precedent*). Even if the result in your case seems preposterous, if the issue has been decided in the past by the court hearing your case or a higher court in your jurisdiction, then the matter is settled. This is the principle of *stare decisis*—you have to follow past precedent. This is true even if you are a judge and don't like the result that will occur.

Law is fundamentally conservative for many reasons, chief of which is so that citizens trying to follow the law will know what to expect. If the law could change at the mere whim of a judge, then society would be so unsettled that people would not know how to behave. Law is also conservative because the *Rule of Law* (meaning a system in which the law will be applied consistently, not according to the inclination of an individual judge) protects litigants from being unfairly treated by judges who dislike them.[2] Finally, the law is conservative for purely practical reasons. If judges were asked to decide anew every legal issue in every case rather than relying on precedent, their workload would be overwhelming and court dockets would grind to a halt. As Supreme Court Justice Louis Brandeis famously explained, "in most matters it is more important that [the question] be settled than that it be decided right."[3]

As you read a case, keep an eye out for a discussion of precedent. This will usually involve the judge citing older cases and comparing them to the decision at hand. The judge will try to explain why the two cases are similar (which means that the precedent *binds* the case at hand and dictates its outcome), or

---

2. For a helpful discussion of the Rule of Law, *see id.* at 10.

3. *Id.* at 43 (quoting *Burnet v. Colorado Oil & Gas Co.,* 285 U.S. 393, 406 (1932) (Brandeis, J., dissenting)).

why they aren't. Think about whether you agree with the judge's analysis. This can be fertile material for professors to ask you about in class.

You should also locate exactly what the court decided in the case, and why. That is the *holding* of the case. Anything else the court said that isn't essential to actually resolving the matter at hand is called *dicta*. The holding of the case is what judges will follow in subsequent cases; the dicta, while informative, is not binding. (For example, the holding of a case might say that the defendant broke the law by driving a car through a public park. The judge might also have spent some time in the decision musing over whether the outcome might have been different had the defendant driven a scooter through the park. But the actual case did not involve a scooter, so this musing would be classed as dicta.)

Many professors will try to get you to apply the case at hand to a hypothetical case that might happen in the future, to see if you understand how the case will work as precedent. If you confront this type of questioning, make sure to pay attention to what the actual holding is, rather than the dicta. Then try to think about what was essential to the holding, and whether those qualities are similar to the hypothetical case that the professor posed to you. If the hypothetical case and the case that you're studying are similar enough, then the case might be a precedent for the hypothetical situation that your professor has imagined. If you can distinguish the two, then it will not bind the subsequent case. (Most professors will think of situations that can be argued either way, and what they want to hear from you is whether you understand what the holding is and how to compare and contrast essential information.)

The Text Matters

Legal analysis can also seem peculiar in the way it emphasizes the exact words of a statute, constitutional provision, or case. A lawyer must always take as his starting point the text of the legal rule or precedent governing his case. Whether you're answering a question in class or before a judge, it is not sufficient to paraphrase the language; very often, the best legal argument will be the one that parses the words the most carefully.

Along the same lines, the judicial system is devoted to adhering strictly to the text of rules. You can see this, for example, in the application of a filing deadline at a courthouse. The rule may say that a brief must be filed by 6 p.m. on a particular day. The original motivation for enacting the rule might have been to keep the employees in the clerk's office from having to work past 7, or to ensure that the brief is on the judge's desk in a timely fashion. You may arrive at the courthouse at 6:05 p.m. and attempt to file your brief, but you'll be turned away. You may argue that there's very little difference between 6 and

6:05; that there was a good reason you were late, because you were saving a child from drowning; that the clerk won't have to work late because you would be happy to walk the brief up to the judge's chambers yourself; but your arguments won't succeed. The rule is clear: 6 p.m. It doesn't matter if the purpose of the rule was or was not implicated, or if you have a good reason why the rule should be bent for you. Clerk's offices are very good at enforcing the rules, and rightfully so. They don't want to be in the business of deciding who has to follow the rules and who should be given an exception — that wouldn't be fair. A clerk's office rule is generally a bright-line rule.

What happens when the text of a rule (or a statute or case) is less clear? Take, for example the text of the Second Amendment of the U.S. Constitution, which says, "A well regulated Militia, being necessary to the security of a free State, the right of the people to keep and bear Arms, shall not be infringed." The text, read literally, seems to draw a connection between the necessity of having a well-regulated militia and the right to bear arms, and so it could be interpreted as saying that people have the right to bear arms if they are going to be part of a militia. But we now understand it to mean that Americans have the right to bear arms, regardless of whether they are serving in a militia (which is what the Supreme Court ultimately decided in *District of Columbia v. Heller*[4]). A typical Socratic dialogue might involve a professor asking one student to take one position about the meaning of the text, and another student to take the opposite position. One student then might rely on the "plain meaning" of the words, while the other might look at the purpose of the provision, how it fits into other parts of the law, what other cases have said about it, and so forth. You might argue based on the letter of the law, or you might argue the intention behind the law. Either way, don't ignore the text as your starting point. Instead, be able to point to particular language to support your argument.

The Importance of Authority

Another peculiarity of legal reasoning is the importance it gives to *authority*, which can be either *binding* (for example, a statute governing the case, or precedent), or *persuasive* (for example, a decision by a court in a different jurisdiction, which a judge is not bound to emulate but does because he believes the reasoning to be true). Pay attention to the hierarchy of the authorities that you rely on when answering questions in class. If you can root your argument in a binding authority, you are on firmer ground than if you were to point to a secondary source, such as a law review article, which may summarize the

---

4. 554 U.S. 570 (2008).

law or argue for changes, but which no judge is required to follow. If you want to rely on non-binding persuasive authority, then you need to be able to articulate why the authority is believable. The more credible the authority (for example, a Nobel-prize-winning scientist who can be trusted to explain scientific principles you don't understand), the more convincing your argument will be.

Using Analogy Well

Lawyers (and law students answering Socratic questions in class) often rely on analogy to make a point. Analogy is a method of arguing in which the speaker points out how the discussed case is similar in some way to a case that has come before it, and therefore concludes that the two cases should be decided in the same way. Note that this isn't always the same thing as precedent — if you can draw an analogy with a case in the same jurisdiction, you may be able to establish that the case is binding, but you can also analogize your case to similar ones that don't exactly govern it, but could still illuminate a fair outcome. To use analogy well, start by laying out the facts of the case that you are studying. (For example: The original case involves a farmer who was held liable for the damage that his cow causes to his neighbor's field; my hypothetical case involves a zookeeper who is being sued because his lion ate a passerby.) Then compare these facts to the hypothetical situation that the professor has posed to you. Emphasize the similarities that are relevant (both involve wild animals that were negligently housed), and discard the ones that are not central to the case (does it matter that one victim was a field and one was a person?). If the cases are similar in central ways, then the cases should result in similar outcomes.[5]

Avoid Logical Fallacies

Many legal arguments are based on the sort of deductive logic that Aristotle spelled out for us long ago — you can figure out the right outcome if you identify the correct legal proposition and apply it to the facts at hand. Aristotle explained this in the form of a *syllogism*, in which a *major premise* and a *minor premise* point the way to a *conclusion* (if A and B are true, then C must be true). His famous example:

---

5. You can read more about the use of analogy in Ruggero J. Aldisert *et al.*, *Logic for Law Students: How to Think Like a Lawyer*, 69 U. Pitt. L. Rev. 1, 16–21 (2007).

> All men are mortal beings.
> Socrates is a man.
> Therefore, Socrates is a mortal being.[6]

Applying this to a modern-day legal example:

> Anyone who takes an item from a store without paying for it has committed larceny.
> John took a necklace from a store without paying for it.
> Therefore, John has committed larceny.

When you read for class, try to identify the *major premise* (the rule of law governing the case), the *minor premise* (the facts particular to your case), and the *conclusion* (the application of the law to the facts). If you do this, you'll be better positioned to talk about the case in class.

Pay particular attention to making sure that your major premise is true. If it isn't, then your conclusion will be flawed. Look at the larceny example again. The common law defines larceny as taking, not "from the person" (meaning not from someone's personal self), with the intent to permanently deprive the owner of the item. Imagine that the store in question was on fire, and John was one of the firefighters who grabbed some valuable items in an effort to save them. The erroneous conclusion that John has committed larceny arises from a misstatement of the major premise. A better analysis of the case would be:

> Anyone who takes an item from a store without paying for it *intending to deprive the owner of it* has committed larceny.
> John took a necklace from a store without paying for it but intended to return it to the owner.
> Therefore, John has not committed larceny.

Aristotle also wrote about the power of *inductive reasoning*, in which a generalized truth is arrived at through observing a series of particular events.[7] This can be a useful sort of argument when it's difficult to prove something; your argument will be more compelling the greater the number of known, observed facts you have, and the more reliable they are. For example, a lawyer might need to argue that a certain kind of medicine does not harm women. She might make this inductive leap by pointing to the example of her sister, who took the medicine in question and was not harmed by it. This would not

---

6. See Edward P.J. Corbett & Robert J. Connors, *Classical Rhetoric for the Modern Student* 38, 42 (4th ed. 1999).

7. *See id.* at 60–61.

be as convincing as an argument based on hundreds of studies showing a similar result.

You will hear many arguments based upon inductive reasoning during your law school classes. If you make such an argument, don't rely only on personal experiences; instead, be sure you can draw upon a large-enough sample from which to generalize. Think about how your sample could be criticized. For example, if your sample is composed of the people sitting around you in class, it's not representative of the population at large, most of whom are not law students.[8] This is how you might attack an expert witness as well—if the sample upon which he bases his opinion is flawed, then his opinion won't be credible.

You can also counter inductive reasoning by pointing out the problem of what psychologists call the *availability heuristic*. This is the phenomenon by which people believe that what they have experienced is typical and predictive of some larger truth, even if their experience is not, in fact, typical at all. For example, if you've just lived through a violent crime or an earthquake, you're more likely to think that something similar will happen again. The event is particularly vivid for you, and therefore seems to have salience, when in fact it might not. This can be a problem with the common law, in which a judge makes law for a large category of disputes based on the concrete case before her, which might not actually be representative of the larger category of cases.[9]

Stay alert for logical fallacies, which can show you the way to attack an opponent's position, or to criticize a judicial opinion. If you avoid them, you won't muck up your own argument.

Strategy Three: Tactical Note-Taking, the One-Page Brief, and Course Outlines

When reading for class, design your notes so that you can use them to help you answer questions. Some students devise a system of taking notes in the margins of their casebooks to help them quickly find the exact language in a case. For example, when I was a law student, I was called on a lot in class during my 1L year. After the experience of fumbling through my notes to find the lan-

---

8. Aldisert, *supra* note 5, at 14–15.
9. Schauer, *supra* note 1, at 110–111.

guage the professor wanted, I began to highlight my casebook strategically. I would write ISSUE (all capital letters) next to the paragraph in the opinion spelling out the problem that the court was solving; HOLDING next to the section laying out the court's decision; and FACTS next to the paragraph that laid out the facts of the case. If the case developed a test, I would write TEST next to that section of the opinion. I would also highlight information that was helpful to one party in yellow, and the information helpful to the other party in pink. I put a box around the most important language of the court's decision. But I was careful not to write too much in my book. I was trying to create a visual aid that I could use to quickly find the things that the professor was most likely to ask me about, and if I wrote too much, I wouldn't be able to find anything quickly.

Here's an example of what I mean. This is the case of *Lucy v. Zehmer*,[10] which you are likely to encounter in your first-year contracts class. (The case is reprinted in the Appendix at the end of this book.) The case involves a dispute about whether Mr. Zehmer actually sold Mr. Lucy his farm, or whether he was just kidding and should not be made to go through with the deal. Figure 1, on the next page, shows the beginning of the case, with the following visual cues on it:

- **PARTIES** (Plaintiff symbolized as π and Defendant symbolized as Δ, which are common abbreviations for these parties)
- **ISSUE** (what the dispute is about)
- **FACTS**, with the facts that help Lucy, the plaintiff, underlined like this, and the facts that help Zehmer, the defendant, highlighted like this

Taking notes in the margins will help you locate the exact language of the court's decision quickly, which can help a great deal in class, because very often the particular language (not a paraphrased version of it) is extremely important.

You should also arm yourself with a *short* (one page or less) write-up of each case that you read. You may have heard of this process described as *briefing* the case. This is not the same thing as a legal brief, which is a lengthy document that a lawyer submits to a court explaining why his client should emerge victorious in some dispute. A case brief for a law school class is a *very short* summary of the important things about the case that you can use when you are discussing it with the professor during a Socratic dialogue.

---

10. 196 Va. 493, 84 S.E.2d 516 (1954). This case is reprinted in the Appendix.

Figure 1: Taking Notes on *Lucy v. Zehmer*

JUDGE: BUCHANAN

BUCHANAN, J., delivered the opinion of the court.

This suit was instituted by W. O. Lucy and J. C. Lucy, complainants, against A. H. Zehmer and Ida S. Zehmer, his wife, defendants, to have specific performance of a contract by which it was alleged the Zehmers had sold to W. O. Lucy a tract of land owned by A. H. Zehmer in Dinwiddie county containing 471.6 acres, more or less, known as the Ferguson farm, for $50,000. J. C. Lucy, the other complainant, is a brother of W. O. Lucy, to whom W. O. Lucy transferred a half interest in his alleged purchase.

— Plaintiff (π)

— Defendant (Δ)

— Issue

The instrument sought to be enforced was written by A. H. Zehmer on December 20, 1952, in these words: 'We hereby agree to sell to W. O. Lucy the Ferguson Farm complete for $50,000.00, title satisfactory to buyer,' and signed by the defendants, A. H. Zehmer and Ida S. Zehmer.

The answer of A. H. Zehmer admitted that at the time mentioned W. O. Lucy offered him $50,000 cash for the farm, but that he, Zehmer, considered that the offer was made in jest; that so thinking, and both he and Lucy having had several drinks, he wrote out 'the memorandum' quoted above and induced his wife to sign it; that he did not deliver the memorandum to Lucy, but that Lucy picked it up, read it, put it in his pocket, attempted to offer Zehmer $5 to bind the bargain, which Zehmer refused to accept, and realizing for the first time that Lucy was serious, Zehmer assured him that he had no intention of selling the farm and that the whole matter was a joke. Lucy left the premises insisting that he had purchased the farm.

Facts that help Lucy

Facts that help Zehmer

Your case brief typically contains the following information:

- Who the parties are
- The issue (stated in a sentence or two to convey the most important legal principles in the case)
- The facts, summarized in about a paragraph

- The procedure, if you are in a class that cares about this
- The rule that is being applied in the case
- The holding (the outcome of the case)
- The reasoning—why the case came out as it did, and what the policy implications are[11]

So your brief for *Lucy v. Zehmer* could look like this:

Lucy v. Zehmer

PARTIES: Plaintiff = Lucy (wants to buy Ferguson farm); Defendant = Zehmer (owns farm)

ISSUE: Does Zehmer have to hand over the farm if he thought the deal was a joke, but acted as if it wasn't? In other words, is a party bound if he acts as if he assents to an agreement, even if he didn't really mean it?

FACTS:

For Zehmer:
- Lucy brought whiskey with him; Zehmer and Lucy were drinking ("high as a Georgia pine")
- A waitress testified that the men were "drinking right much"
- Zehmer says he thought this was all a joke
- Zehmer whispered to his wife that it was a joke
- The conversation sounded as if it was in jest (Lucy: "I bet you wouldn't take $50K for that place." Zehmer: "Yes, I would too; you wouldn't give $50.")
- Zehmer wrote out the contract on the back of a restaurant check—very informal
- Zehmer refused to take Lucy's $5 to bind the bargain, saying, "This is liquor talking. I don't want to sell the farm."
- Zehmer sent Lucy a letter saying he'd never agreed to sell

For Lucy:
- Lucy had tried to buy place before—clearly he wanted it
- Zehmer actually put the contract in writing—wrote it himself
- The contract states, "We hereby agree to sell to W.O. Lucy the Ferguson Farm complete for $50,000.00, title satisfactory to buyer." Clear terms.
- Zehmer re-wrote the contract, changing it from "I" to We" when Lucy pointed out that Mrs. Zehmer would need to sign it, too

---

11. For a humorous description of case briefing and creating a course outline, *see* Austin L. Parrish & Cristina C. Knolton, *Hard-Nosed Advice From a Cranky Law Professor* 19–34, 47–57 (2010).

- Both Zehmers signed the contract
- The discussion about the contract was lengthy (30–40 minutes)
- Lucy did not feel drunk, and said Zehmer did not seem drunk
- Lucy immediately arranged financing and checked title

HOLDING: Zehmer acted like he wanted to sell, so it doesn't matter what he was really thinking. Zehmer has to convey the farm to Lucy.

REASONING: There was an offer, acceptance, execution, and delivery of the written contract. The law doesn't require the "mental assent of the parties"—what Zehmer thought doesn't matter if Lucy didn't know what he was thinking. Reason for the policy: if you could get out of a contract by saying that you didn't really mean it, then all contracts would be unenforceable. (Note that you could argue that Lucy did know that Zehmer didn't mean to sell, since Lucy brought in the whiskey and encouraged him to drink, which sounds like an effort to trick him. One could argue that this rewards devious behavior on Lucy's part. Court deals with this by saying they weren't drinking much and that there isn't evidence of fraud.)

A case brief like this one would help you a great deal if you were called on in class. You would be able to argue on behalf of either Lucy or Zehmer because you went to the trouble of splitting the facts into two categories (the ones that help Lucy and the ones that help Zehmer), putting them into a list that's a lot easier to follow than the highlighted case would be. You've included the exact language where it matters (such as the language of the contract). You could also find the exact language of important parts of the case if you had to by referring to the highlighting that you did in the casebook itself. And in the process of creating the case brief, you have figured out the significance of the case, plus the best argument against the court if you want to take the position that it came out the wrong way.

Notice that to write this brief, you've had to make choices. For example, the issue is described in this brief as, "Is a party bound if he acts as if he assents to an agreement, even if he didn't really mean it?" It could have been described as, "Whether W. O. Lucy and J. C. Lucy can have specific performance of a contract by which it was alleged the Zehmers had sold to W. O. Lucy a tract of land owned by A. H. Zehmer in Dinwiddie County containing 471.6 acres, more or less, known as the Ferguson Farm, for $50,000." That tracks the actual language of the case. But it's a lot more difficult to process mentally and to say aloud in class. Plus, despite this language, the case doesn't really focus very much on "specific performance" (which means making Zehmer turn over the property versus, say, paying Lucy some damages)—the court asks whether there was a contract in the first place and spends no time at all asking whether specific performance would be the appropriate remedy. The fact that the farm is called Ferguson Farm, and is 471.6 acres in size, and that Lucy offered $50,000 for it, are also largely irrelevant here. The things that are more relevant—Zehmer's whisper to his wife that it's a joke, Lucy's bottle of whiskey, the written agreement on the restaurant receipt—are the points you should include in your case brief. Leave the rest out.

Many of the students I interviewed for this book tried their hands at case briefing, and they all came up with their own ways to do it. The brief I have supplied is the model that I used in law school, but yours doesn't have to look like this. It's helpful, though, to develop a template for your case briefs and follow it so you can quickly find what you're looking for if you are called on in class. Keep your case briefs short so that you aren't distracted by extraneous information. Bullet-point lists can help you find answers quickly as well.

The "policy/reasoning" part of the case brief is often the most important thing that you'll write. Again and again, the students I interviewed talked about spending the most time on teasing this out of the cases they read. Before you read, look at the syllabus to figure out where the case fits into the course generally before you read it, and then determine how the case advances the topic that you're studying. What are the consequences of the decision? Why was it right (or wrong)? What were the steps that the court took to make the decision, and did any of those steps require questionable assumptions? Think through what you would ask if you were the professor teaching the case—those are the questions that you are most likely to get in class. (You might also look at the questions posed in the notes section that many textbooks include at the end of each chapter. Especially during your first semester, when you are getting the hang of figuring out what is important in a case, these questions can point you in the right direction.)

The process of writing the case brief lets you internalize the case. It's a way to learn. If you've taken the time to read the case twice, to highlight the case sparingly and create margin notes, and then to summarize it again in a case brief, then you've given yourself the time you will need to really understand the material. You will have gone through it several times and thought about it from different angles. That's a different way of reading from the speed-reading that might have gotten you through college. It's much more akin to the kind of close, careful reading that you will be doing every day as an attorney.

Once you are three or four weeks into the semester, it can be helpful to start a course outline. A course outline is a document that *you write yourself* that lets you see the big picture of how the cases are connected to one another. You could buy commercial outlines or borrow one from a friend, but simply reading someone else's outline does not help you master the material. You have to go through the steps of putting the outline together yourself to get something out of it. Very often, a professor will let you use your course outline during the exam, and that can be helpful, but exams are so fast-paced that you probably won't have time to look up everything on your outline. You need to already know it—to have made the connections yourself already, so that you aren't thinking things through for the first time while the exam clock is ticking. That's why borrowing an outline from a classmate doesn't work—you won't really know every little thing that's in there because you didn't write it yourself. You need to see how the cases connect, and your professor may not spell it out for you in class. It's your job to make those connections. That work is essential to learning to be a lawyer.

The headers of each section of your outline should line up with what your professor has written on the syllabus, or you could use the chapter headings of your textbook. Then put your case briefs into the outline. Link the briefs with a sentence or two about how it all fits together. At the end of each week, update your outline with the material that you have covered that week. If you do this, your answers to Socratic questioning will improve immeasurably because you (unlike some of your classmates) will be able to put new lessons in context and link them to the big picture. When the class ends, you will have already internalized a lot of the material, and you'll have a document in hand that will help you greatly on the exam. The outline also offers a checklist of sorts for exam questions. You can look at each section of the outline, figure out whether it applies, and follow it to the answer that the professor is looking for.

Now that you have a plan for tackling the reading, some sense of what to look for, and a note-taking method, let's turn to how to use these materials during class.

Chapter Three

The Socratic Method: Strategies in the Classroom

You've done the reading and taken careful, strategic notes. The morning of class arrives. Now what?

Strategy One: Pay Attention in Class

The Socratic Method is based on the assumption that you learn the law not just from the reading you do before class, but by playing with that reading during class. That means you have to pay attention to what's going on. Every day. Even if you are not the student on call.

Position yourself so that you are more likely to pay attention. Many of the students who spoke with me complained of the distractions of the Internet—either because their friends sent them messages, or because they couldn't resist surfing, or because they found themselves looking over their neighbor's shoulders to see what websites they were browsing when they should have been paying attention to the conversation going on in class. Allowing yourself to be distracted during class is a huge mistake. Think of it this way: Law school is extremely expensive. Students who attend top law schools may pay more than $70,000 each year—that's $210,000 over the course of their studies—in tuition, fees, and living expenses. Law school class time is *not* when you should be shopping on Zappos. You have paid a huge amount of money to learn to think like a lawyer. You owe it to yourself (and your family, if they are helping you) to actually do the work that will teach you to think like a lawyer. That means focusing during class.

Several students told me that they don't bring laptops to class, simply to avoid the temptations of the Internet. This can be a wise strategy for other reasons as well. When you have a laptop, you're likely able to type quickly enough to transcribe most of the class, without actually thinking about what you're writing. Try taking notes with a pen and paper instead. You'll find that you have to be more selective about the notes you take—forcing you to *think* and engage with the material before you write. When you're an attorney, you will also find that having a computer between you and your client keeps you from being able to connect with him, and can be off-putting. Many attorneys make it a rule to take notes with pen and paper because it is less obtrusive. Law school is a good time to practice this skill.

Consider sitting near the front of the room. You can't be distracted by classmates' online surfing if you can't see their computer screens. You'll also be more likely to ask questions or participate in the discussion if you are closer to the professor. Plus it's easier to hear from the front of the room, so you won't miss anything. After class, you'll be better positioned to approach the professor, which can help you develop a relationship with her that could lead to a recommendation letter later. If you are worried your classmates will think you're a "gunner" for sitting up front, remember that $210,000 law school loan burden. Get your money's worth. I guarantee you, no one will remember where you sat after the semester is over. Don't let a less-than-ideal classroom keep you from leaning.

Even if you find yourself in a class you think is poorly organized, you can learn the skills you need to be a fine lawyer. Be your own law professor. Decide for yourself whether a classmate's answer was well reasoned, and make yourself figure out why. As one student, Steven, told me: "I think a lot of people, when they don't hear their name, are so grateful that they're not the one called on that they just don't even think about what other people are doing. They're just thanking their lucky stars they dodged the bullet. But it's helpful to listen to the conversation." If you pay attention to the professor's response, you can begin to see what he or she is looking for on the exam.

Students sometimes get frustrated when they believe that the conversation in class has been hijacked by classmates and seems to go nowhere. It's a common complaint in course evaluations that the professor didn't guide the conversation properly, or provide a "wrap" at the end of class. Some professors *are* better than others at guiding a conversation, but it's also true that many classroom discussions are meant to be more about the exploration than the resolution of a legal quandary. Law can sometimes be resolved in a variety of ways; the goal of law school is to help you see those possibilities.

Strategy Two: Techniques for Answering the Question

Though preparation is essential for doing well in class, "performance" is another part of handling the Socratic Method that you can learn and improve upon, as Jeree, a recent graduate, realized during her time at law school.

Jeree describes herself as "extremely shy in high school and even in the beginning of college." The Socratic Method terrified her at first: "My first year I would get nervous and feel the need to fill the silence with filler noises, rambling or mumbling. My assumption was always that the material was perfectly clear and I just was not getting it."

Jeree is precisely the kind of student whom Harvard law professor and noted civil rights scholar Lani Guinier warned in *Becoming Gentlemen*[1] could have been marginalized by her law school experience. Guinier's seminal 1997 study of the experiences of women at the University of Pennsylvania Law School found that the hierarchical, competitive environment of the law school classroom intimidates and silences many women and students of color. These students may internalize mistakes and begin to question their own abilities.[2] Guinier and her colleagues noted that male students were more likely than female students to speak in class, receive more attention from their professors, and find that their remarks are accepted by their peers.[3]

Jeree — naturally self-effacing, and an African-American woman in a school where roughly 75 percent of the students are white and 55 percent of the students are male — initially didn't want to speak up in class out of fear that she would say something wrong. Ironically, a professor who used the Socratic Method very aggressively helped her conquer this fear:

> My first year, I had a professor who called on me quite a bit and I think the reason why he did it was to break me of my fear. He could tell from my overly expressive face that I always had something to say, but I would not always raise my hand and say it. Once I realized that one wrong answer, mistake, or stumble was not the end of the world, I gained a greater sense of confidence in answering cold calls.

Jeree benefitted from practice. Because her professor wouldn't let her off the hook, she was able to practice answering questions over and over again, and the more she did it, the better she got.

She soon realized her initial assumption that her struggles with the material were due to some failure on her part was wrong: "I realized the material is not always perfectly clear, which is why there are law review articles, books, and cases analyzing the topic." She began to explore different techniques for preparing for class:

---

1. Lani Guinier *et al*, *Becoming Gentlemen: Women, Law School, and Institutional Change* 8–9 (1997).

2. *Id.* at 2–3.

3. *Id.* at 12–13, 50.

When I started to realize that professors are not just interested in what the casebook says, but also in what I think, it changed the way I prepared for class. To prepare, I ask myself questions about the case. I ask myself if I would decide the case the way that the judge decided the case. I look at the location and the time period of the case or material and ask if there is some historical or regional significance to the opinion. The best thing that I learned how to do was become my own law professor. After 1L year, I learned to think about the sort of things that are not in the text that the professor might ask about the reading. I began to think more about how the assignment connects to the material and theoretical frameworks of the course.

Jeree also started considering what she could do to have a more positive outcome during the questioning itself. She could see that answering questions day after day in class was improving her performance, so she sought out other places where she could practice. She signed up for a variety of oral advocacy classes in law school, which helped hone her verbal skills, and the feedback she received in those courses also helped her improve. Jeree also took leadership roles in student organizations that required her to speak in front of peers and professionals.

Jeree's abilities soared, and by the time she graduated, she was beloved by many professors who praised her participation in class. She received two prestigious awards during her third year of law school: a public service law fellowship that allowed her to work after graduation at a legal aid office to assist incarcerated youths, and an award recognizing her as one of the most outstanding members of her law school class.

Jeree developed a technique for managing stress during cold calls, which she calls "TBA": "I learned to embrace the silence. Embracing the silence and taking the time to think about what I am going to say is one of the techniques that I use. TBA—Think, Breathe, and Answer."

Other students reported that they use a similar strategy. As second-year student Caitlin said, "I try to take a minute to think before I respond, because it's easy to trap yourself by speaking without considering the implications of your statement first, especially if you're working with a hypothetical." If you need a moment to think, take it.

It's also important to make sure you understand what the professor is asking you. Kent, a third-year student, said, "I really try to listen to what's being asked of me and actually answer the question instead of deciding that I don't know that answer and then trying to answer a slightly different question. I'll ask for clarification if I don't understand what the question is." If you don't understand the question, there is no shame in asking the professor to rephrase it.

You don't need to wait passively for a professor to call on you if you have something to say in class. You may already have figured out that if you volunteer in class, you are less likely to be cold-called because the professor has already heard from you. This does not guarantee that you will not be cold-called, because professors are wise to this game and know that some students try to volunteer in order to head off the surprise questions. But very often it works. If you want to volunteer in class, don't take too long to perfect the idea. If you do, your comment may not be relevant any longer because the class has moved on. It's more important to contribute the idea than it is to make it perfect.

Do, however, consider the appropriateness of the comment or question. If you ask a question that is idiosyncratic and takes the conversation off course, your classmates may resent you for taking up class time. These questions are better left to after-class discussions with the professor. Similarly, if you constantly interrupt class with questions—if you raise your hand to offer a thought at each class meeting—both your classmates and the professor will tire of you quickly. But if you haven't already hogged too much airtime and you have a question that goes to the heart of the class, then it can be extremely helpful to everyone for you to ask it.

As you volunteer an answer or respond to the surprise question, give some thought to the tone you use. Striking the right tone can make all the difference in persuading an audience, and is a skill you'll use constantly once you become a lawyer. It can be startling to be called on in class, and a professor's aggressive questioning understandably may make you feel defensive. Try to quash that feeling and respond as if the exchange is simply a conversation, not a battle of wits. Says third-year student Ginny, "When I've done well, it's been when I've been able to keep a more conversational tone, instead of feeling more threatened, like, 'Oh my gosh, he's asking me a question and I don't know what's going on.'" Steven, a second-year law student, agrees:

> Socratic dialogue shouldn't be a battle between you and the professor, because they're on your side—they're trying to advance the goals of [the course]. Think of it as collaborative: You're passing me the ball so I can pass it back to you. This is a lot better than if you think, 'I've got to conquer him. I've got to present some brilliant insight that this professor has never heard.' I mean, that's never gonna happen. The people are the top of their field. You're never going to outdo them.

Other students (and professors, too) struggle with the problem of sounding arrogant when they speak in class. Your goal in speaking is not to expound upon a case, or to show off your intellectual abilities. It's simply to move the ball forward in discussion. Beware of taking yourself too seriously. Your class-room persona is the beginning of your reputation as a lawyer, and classmates often remember (and ridicule) the colleague who sounded pompous as a 1L. Be extremely careful of sounding dismissive of your classmates' ideas, because those classmates will remember those exchanges for a long, long time. You can disagree with people without eye-rolling or derision. Don't laugh at any-one. Law students sometimes copy the snarky tone of political debates on TV because they lack good examples, but pundits and politicians don't model the most persuasive tone. A better tone would be one that shows an earnest col-laboration between equals. Your classmates will become your colleagues once you enter the workforce, so you should care about what they think of you, in-cluding what they think of your in-class behavior. (See Chapter Four for a more detailed discussion of the importance of ethos, or credibility.) For these same reasons, it's a good idea to make some friends in law school, and to be generous to classmates who are struggling or who have different views on an issue. Be polite in classroom exchanges and share your notes when asked out-side of class.

On the opposite end of the spectrum, try to avoid sounding too self-depre-cating or fearful when you speak in class. If you end every sentence with a ques-tion mark, or mumble, or trail off as if you are unsure, then the professor and your classmates are less likely to take your ideas seriously. It's perfectly fine — normal, in fact — to feel nervous. But practice masking that nervousness, be-cause you'll be called on time and again during your legal career to project con-fidence on behalf of a client, even if you don't feel it. Law school is the perfect time to acquire that ability. Speak loudly, slowly, and clearly. Look the professor in the eye and don't use garbage words ("like") or filler sounds ("um"). Don't play with your hair or cock your head, and don't undercut the strength of what you've just said by trailing off or turning a statement into a question (by in-flecting your voice upward).

Many of the students to whom I spoke mentioned the importance of tone, and modeled the behavior in their conversations with me. I could see that they might be doing well in class because they all seemed attuned to the subtleties of human conversation — not sounding too self-important, or alternatively, too uncertain. If you put forth an idea with an air of confidence that doesn't stray into the realm of hubris, your audience is likely to give your thoughts more weight.

Strategy Three: What to Do If You Don't Know the Answer

If the professor asks you a question and you think you don't know the answer, try this strategy:

- If you are truly unprepared because you have not done the reading for the day, say so. Don't waste the class's time. Then make sure that you do the reading for that class religiously thereafter, or at least until you have been called upon again and answered correctly.
- If you have done the reading, then take a deep breath. This is simply a conversation between you and the professor about what you've read. Take a moment to think before you speak.
- Listen to the question. If you don't understand it, ask for clarification. There's nothing wrong about asking the professor to rephrase what he or she is asking. That can give you time to think.
- Answer the question to the best of your abilities.
- Some professors push you the most on the things you are right about. Don't take follow-up questions as an indicator that you have done something wrong. Use them as a chance to expand your brain. Think. Answer.
- Slow down. If you start talking fast, it's hard to think straight.
- Trust yourself. Many students know the right answers but are too intimidated to share them. You were smart enough to get into law school. Keep using the skills that got you here.
- Mentally lower the stakes. Truthfully, no one is likely to remember the details of the colloquy after it's over, not even the professor. In your mind, think to yourself, "I am just answering a question," which is something that you have done millions of times in the past. Feeling nervous is natural, but don't let that stop you from speaking. And everyone in the room has been in the same position as you—including the professor. People are much more likely to be feeling sympathy for you than to be judging you.
- Keep your tone in mind—including how it might sound to the professor.

The following is an imaginary exchange from a criminal law class in which the student finds herself understandably flustered. She tries to lighten the mood by cracking a joke—a mistake with this type of professor. But notice how she's able to regain her footing by soldiering on with her answers. Even if you feel horribly embarrassed, just keep going. Most professors will be patient with you so long as you seem prepared, even if you are struggling.

Professor: Ms. Jones.... Please recite the facts of *Regina v. Faulkner.*[4]

Student: [Looking startled, ruffles her notes and books, and attempts to compose herself.] Mr. Faulkner was traveling ... on a rum ship and went below to drink ... to steal some rum. Then he lit a match to see in the dark hold, and the ship exploded.

Professor: And why was he on the ship?

Student: [Flustered.] I'm not sure? He was a sailor ...

Professor: Yes. However, this is still unclear to me. If he was a sailor on the ship, why would he not be allowed to drink the rum?

Student: Well, it wasn't his rum. It was cargo that the ship was transporting.

Professor: Correct. So it wasn't his rum, but he went to drink it anyway?

Student: Yes.

Professor: Why would he do that?

Generally a bad idea to crack a joke if your professor seems grouchy that day.

Student: [Grasping for any answer.] Well, I guess he was thirsty? [Class laughs.]

Professor: [Not looking the least bit amused.] So he went down into the bulkhead of the *Zemindar*, into forecastle hold where the rum was being stored, opened a casket of rum—rum for which he had no obvious authority to drink—simply because he was thirsty? Please do not bother to answer that question, Ms. Jones; because the obvious answer is that he did not. Perhaps I should make this easier for you. To whom did the rum belong?

This is the sort of information you should have highlighted in your casebook.

Student: [Panicking now, she flips to the first page of the case and luckily finds the answer; with a slight sigh of relief, she says:] Sandback, Tenne, and Company.

---

4. 13 Cox Crim. Case 550 (1877). You can read the opinion in the Appendix at the end of the book.

Professor: So then I ask you again: Why would Seaman Faulkner go into the forecastle hold of the *Zemindar*?

Student: To ... to ... I guess to steal Sandback's rum?

Professor: You guess? Ms. Jones, I would like to point out that we're not playing a guessing game here. The Crown is seeking to impose seven years of penal servitude on Mr. Faulkner. Please restate your answer.

Student: [Mustering up confidence, her voice still shaking from uncertainty.] To steal ... Sandback's rum.

Professor: Thank you. So you are saying that Seaman Faulkner went into the hold with the deliberate thought of taking rum that was not his?

Student: [Considering recanting, but deciding to move forward.] Yes. He knew what he was doing ...

Professor: "He knew what he was doing." [Tension builds in the silent pause; the entire class is aware of another misstep.] Did he know that the ship would explode?

Student: No ... no, he did not. [Beginning to catch on.] Well, he had the requisite *mens rea*.... I think the court says ... the court says he went into the hold with the purpose to steal the rum. So he knew what he was doing. I guess ... I guess ... I mean, whether he knew the ship would explode ... it's difficult to say. Nothing in the facts suggests that he wanted to blow up the ship; he just wanted some rum. But then, he lit a match near alcohol in a small, enclosed area. It's hard to say. I mean he hurt himself in the act. I don't think he would have lit the match if he knew it would explode.... This wasn't a suicide mission. Faulkner just wanted the rum. It seems more like he just wasn't thinking.... He was being reckless.

This is a good answer. An important concept in the case is that Faulkner knew that he was stealing the rum, but did not know this would destroy the ship. The only problem: "Reckless" may not be what the student actually means.

Professor: [Pleased at Ms. Jones's answer, the professor lets up.] Reckless?

Student: [Swings, and hits the next pitch.] No.... not reckless. I mean, he didn't know the ship would explode and then ignored that risk. He just wasn't aware of the risk. He was being negligent.

The term "reckless" has a specific legal meaning, so the student should be careful when she uses it. She realizes her mistake here and switches to the correct term, which is "negligent."

Professor: A fine piece of lawyerly analysis, Ms. Jones. What did the jury find?

Student: The jury ... the jury found Seaman Faulkner guilty on the count of larceny for stealing Sandback's rum, and also guilty on the count of arson for the fire that destroyed the ship. The judge directed that, should the jury find Faulkner to have the *mens rea* for the theft, that such a *mens rea* would be sufficient to find him guilty for the fire.

Professor: Do you agree with that reasoning?

Student: Well, on appeal ...

Always listen to the question.

Professor: I'm not asking you what happened on appeal, Ms. Jones. Please answer the question.

Student: No ... no, I don't agree with the reasoning.... I think ... it seems to me that the fire was much more serious than the theft. I mean it takes a certain mindset to commit yourself to stealing, and then it takes a certain mindset to destroy a boat. While I think Faulkner had the intent—the purpose—to steal rum that wasn't his, he didn't have the intent to blow up the ship. It was an accident. I don't think he should be punished for an accident that the person didn't foresee. It doesn't seem very fair.

Professor: But maybe we want to further discourage criminal actions by punishing for the unintended consequences of a criminal act?

This is a good answer.

Student: That could be a viable alternative ... I guess. But it still doesn't seem fair to Faulkner. Why should he be punished the same as someone who deliberately blows up a ship? Certainly that person is more dangerous to society ... and ... and should be punished more harshly.

Professor: Is the goal of criminal law to punish according to dangerousness to society?

Student: One of the goals, certainly. I would argue it is one of the main goals.

Professor: Allowing for your assumption, I will accept your argument. Please tell me then, what do the judges hold on appeal?

Student: Each one?

Professor: Actually, no. Please just tell me what Judge Barry holds.

Student: Judge Barry cites the ... I think it was a statute that said that the actual act must be intentional and willful, unless the ... unless Faulkner was aware of the consequence and went through with the act anyway. He thinks that ... he thinks that the instructions to the jury were erroneous and that the jury must find that Faulkner had the appropriate *mens rea* for the arson. I guess ... I mean, essentially holding that the jury must determine if Faulkner was aware of the potential fire, or if he intended to cause it.

Correct answer. This is something the student should have highlighted in the casebook.

Professor: Thank you, Ms. Jones ... [Looks around the room.] Mr. Doe! [Mr. Doe jumps.]

Strategy Four: Learn to Overcome Self-Consciousness

Kent was a rising 3L when I spoke to him, and had just been named the editor-in-chief of the Virginia Law Review. He was an academic superstar with an understated confidence, so it might surprise 1Ls who meet him to know that during his first year of law school, he worried that he was out of place:

> When I first got here, I really struggled with whether I belonged here at all. That made me really nervous [in class] because I was coming from a music background, [and] because I hadn't gone to an Ivy League college like so many of my classmates. As a musician, the type of work that I did just wasn't academically strenuous. It was more performance-based and practicing- and skills-based, so for those reasons I was always worried. I didn't have a political science or history background, so I always felt like there was just this level of knowledge that everyone had that I didn't have. It took me a while to work through that.

But even though Kent had no previous law experience, or any public speaking experience, he found that his undergraduate degree in music served him well in class. He learned as a singer that you cannot be self-conscious if you want to succeed. At some point, you have to trust yourself:

> I learned when I used to perform that if I listen to every sound that's coming out of my mouth as I am singing, then I'll be constantly judging myself and there will be no artistry; there will be no music. It's the same thing with speaking in class. If you're constantly considering what you just said, you can't be thinking about what you're currently saying.

Kent knew how to develop the sort of thick skin that a performer needs to be able to go onstage before an audience, and applied this same ability to his performance in class. The most important trick, he says, is to keep going.

> Feeling nervous or even being embarrassed or even saying something stupid is just a momentary bad feeling that fades. It's not something that's awful or something that's terrible forever. It passes very quickly, and it happens to everybody and the sooner you can get used to it, the better off you're going to be.

Other students echoed Kent's advice about achieving confidence, which they were able to hone through their own personal interests and activities. Said Steven,

> I'm a pretty chatty person to begin with. I worked in politics for three years before coming to law school, on a political campaign. My job description was to talk to people. I think a good cold call is like playing a game of badminton—batting it back and forth—and if you're completely self-conscious, it is difficult to do that.

Ginny's confidence came from participating in small-group classes in college:

> I went to a really, really small high school and I went to a small college. Before I came to law school, I'd never been in a class bigger than 30 students in my life. The classes in college were really conversational and it wasn't stigmatizing to talk in class or volunteer because if you have a class with eight people and no one is volunteering, then it's just awkward. I also worked for three years between college and law school on smallish teams, so there would be a lot of situations where there were four to 10 people around a conference table sitting around talking, and you're expected to contribute. You've done the work, there's information that each person's worked on that they need to share with the team, so it's natural to discuss it.

For Kara, confidence came from parents who expected her to interact with adults, and also from public speaking classes:

> This might sound corny, but I grew up with a politician for a father and always loved going to political events with him since I was a young child. So at an early age I had to get used to speaking intelligently with adults (or at least trying to) in fairly uncomfortable situations. Seeing him give campaign and other speeches very often also probably inspired me to care about public speaking more than the average young person. I have also been asked to give speeches (once to a crowd of over a thousand) because of my background as a cancer survivor and fundraiser, which was difficult but really helped me as a public speaker in general. And finally, I took a brief public speaking course in high school; I don't remember much

from it but know that it helped me get over the initial paralyzing nerves, which has always been my biggest challenge with speaking.

If you lack experience with performance, debate, or discussion-based classes and if you are not naturally extroverted, don't despair. Each one of these confident students described times in which they felt uncomfortable speaking in a group, but also talked about how they were able to master the skill by calling on what they'd learned in other areas of their lives. Law school offers a wonderful opportunity for you to enroll in seminars, public speaking classes, trial practice classes, and clinics that require you to practice articulating your ideas aloud. If you struggle with the Socratic Method, consider finding one of these small-group classes that require in-class participation, because they can offer you the practice you need to get better.

Strategy Five: Predict the Questions

The following is a list of the types of things you are likely to be asked in a Socratic colloquy. You can use them to help you prepare for class.

Facts

- Who are the parties?
- What does the appellant want? What is the remedy being sought?
- What are the facts of the case?
- Do you agree with how the court has characterized the facts of the case?
- What is the definition of [jargon word/legal doctrine]?

Procedure

- What was the lower court's holding?
- What's the standard of review?[5] Who has the burden of persuasion/proof?[6]

Issues in Dispute

- What's at issue here? Why are we in court?
- What are the parties' disagreements?
- What are the broader issues implicated by the specific facts of the case?

---

5. The *standard of review* is the amount of deference that a reviewing court must give to a lower court's decision.

6. The party with the *burden of persuasion or proof* is the side that has to prove the elements of a claim in order to win. For example, in a criminal case, the government bears the burden of proving the defendant guilty, but the defendant is not required to prove himself innocent. If the government cannot meet its burden, the defendant goes free.

Rule
- What was the legal rule/standard applied?
- What were the elements/factors of the rule described?
- What are the alternative/minority rules?

Holding
- What's the holding?/What's the outcome?/What does the judge rule?
- What were the judge's reasons for the holding?
- How does this reasoning differ from the lower court's reasoning?
- Is the court's reasoning persuasive? Has the court considered all arguments? Are there better arguments?

Policy
- Do you agree with the judge's reasoning and holding?
- Does this holding conflict with some other legal rule or case?
- Given the facts at play, is the law/rule that was applied the best way to reach the desired social/political/economic effect? Is there a better rule?
- What are the social/political/economic effects of the decision?
- What are the implications/future effects of the rule/holding of this case?
- Which side is more at fault? Who could have prevented the harm/dispute?

Arguments
- What did the plaintiff/appellant argue?
- What did the defendant/appellee argue?
- What is each judge's reasoning for his or her holding?
- What are the strengths and weaknesses of each argument (for the appellant/appellee or in comparing the arguments made by the judges)?

Hypotheticals
- If the facts where changed [in a certain way], would the result be the same?
- If an alternative [specific] rule were applied to the facts, what would be the outcome?
- Given [a certain set of facts], what is the best rule to apply?
- How can [this case] be reconciled with [a different case]?
- How can [this case] be distinguished from [a similar case]?

Role-Play
- Imagine you are the appellant or appellee. Make the best argument to convince the court to rule in your favor.
- Imagine you are the judge. Would you rule the same way?
- [After listening to two students each argue a side of a case] Who should win and why?

Past Standards/Doctrines Applied to Case

- Considering this case, would [prior case read] be decided differently?
- Can the same holding be reached by applying [alternative doctrine]?

Read Between the Lines

- Are the intentions of the parties different from what they claim?
- Consider the facts left out, or likely facts given the situation that are *not* stated, and answer [this question].
- Consider whether the court is justifying its holding in order to avoid certain unfavorable implications of an alternative holding.

One final tip—sometimes, if you listen carefully to the questions, you can figure out exactly how the professor wants you to answer, a skill that you will also use in some interactions with supervisors and even judges. Here is one last Socratic exchange to illustrate the point. This one takes place in a Property class.

Professor: *Hilder v. St. Peter*[7].... Let me pull up the facts here. [Delay as the professor pulls up a PowerPoint with the main facts of the case listed in bullet points.] *Hilder v. St. Peter*. So we have the apartment that's nearly falling apart ... Who hasn't been called on yet? [Some students raise their hands.] Still haven't got everyone.... Okay. Mr. Smith! What do you think this apartment should rent for?

Student: Well, Hilder agreed to pay St. Peter $140 a month for the apartment.

Professor: Okay—$140 per month. [Writes the dollar amount on the board.] Do you think this apartment is worth more?

Student: [Confused.] Umm ... [Pauses for a while. Then the professor starts shaking his head.] Nooo ... [In response to the professor's lead.]

Professor: Good! How do we know that it's not worth more? [Slight pause.] Because if it were, then St. Peter would have rented it for more! So we have this apartment that's falling apart and St. Peter can only get $140 for it,

---

7. 478 A.2d 202, 144 Vt. 150 (1984). You can read this case in the Appendix.

so he rents it to Hilder for $140. Then Hilder sues him because ... so why does Hilder sue him?

Good answer, and the sort of information the student should have highlighted when doing the reading.

Student: Well, the apartment is falling apart. Let's see [looks to the book] ... the door wouldn't lock, there was water leaking from the ceiling, and there was a raw sewage odor.

Professor: So Hilder sues St. Peter to fix the apartment under this implied warranty of habitability. Let's look at this closer [draws a diagram of a small street on the board].... Over here we have St. Peter's apartment with all its problems. Across the street we have another apartment, but this is perfectly up to code. How much do you think this one rents for?

Student: Umm ... $200.

Professor: No. Let me tell you. [Laughs.] This one rents for a hell of a lot more than $200. Let's say $500. Let's call this Jones's Apartments. Then down here [draws another apartment on the board, adding to the neighborhood] ... down here is Smith's Apartments. They are also falling apart, so how much do you think they rent for?

Good answer.

Student: Probably the same as St. Peter's ... so $140.

Professor: Yeah, $140. [Writes the dollar amounts next to the apartments on the board. Points back to St. Peter's apartment.] So this apartment here ... this apartment is renting for $140, but how much does the court say it's worth? [Pauses.]

Student: Uhh ...

Professor: [Helpful.] Let me rephrase. So how much in damages does the court award for the breach of the implied warranty?

Student: I think the court awards ... it says here the court awards $4,945.

Professor: Okay. Well some of that is for compensatory damages, which don't really make sense and seemed to come out of thin air at the trial court. So ignoring that, what does the court award?

Student: $3,445. The entire rent.

Professor: The entire rent! So what does the court think this apartment [points to St. Peter's apartment on the board] is worth in the state that it's in?

Student: Nothing. Zero … I guess.

Good answer.

Professor: Does Hilder still get to use the apartment during the time it is in disrepair?

Student: Yes …

Professor: Do you think it's worth zero?

Student: No. I mean it's got to be worth something because people are still living there … it's not worth zero. That would mean it has no use to anyone.

Good answer.

Professor: So what's it worth?

Student: [Brief pause.] Uhh …

Professor: It's worth $140! That's what Hilder is paying for it. That's probably market. So here is usually what happens in places like this. Apartment complexes usually have different stages of use … usually five stages. What happens is when these apartments fall into disrepair, the owners abandon them. That's stage five. What do you think happens in stage five?

This is a debatable point, but it's a fair assumption.

Student: They are condemned?

Professor: Yes, condemned and destroyed.... So St. Peter's and Smith's Apartments are in, like, stage four. But then the court requires St. Peter to fix his apartment and bring it up to code under the court-constructed implied warranty of habitability. What do you think happens after the court orders this?

Student: Well, I guess then St. Peter would charge more for his apartment?

Professor: Yes. How much would he charge now?

Student: Probably around $500, the price for an apartment fully up to code … like the one across the street.

Good answer.

Professor: Right. So this apartment that Hilder was renting for $140 is now worth $500. And how much is the lease contract for?

Student: $140 a month.

Professor: Do you think St. Peter would have rented the apartment for $140 to Hilder if it was fully up to code?

Student: Probably not.

Professor: Right. Probably not. So the court forces St. Peter to fully repair the apartment up to code, and Hilder's lease is up. How much does he go to rent the apartment for now?

Student: $500.

Professor: And where does Hilder go now?

Student: Umm ... she pays St. Peter the $500?

Professor: Noooo! If she could afford to pay St. Peter the $500, do you think she would have rented the dump in the first place, or do you think she would have gone across the street to rent from Jones?

Student: I guess she would have rented from Jones?

Professor: Yeah, she can't afford that. And now she can't afford St. Peter's either. So she rents from Smith. And what happens? This time she doesn't take her problems to court, and she can continue to pay the $140.... See, the implied warranty of habitability actually hurts the very people it's trying to help. This is not a problem of housing. It is a problem of substandard incomes. If all the apartments are brought up to code, people like Hilder have no place to live that they can afford. [Rhetorically.] So what do we see happening? We see these problems not brought to court. We see people in these complexes alienating those that bring these problems to court because it forces everyone out of the apartments once they are repaired. And then you have these legal aid places ... these places urge tenants to bring the cases to court ... because then they get work. They bring these cases in and then the only people they are hurting are their clients! The implied warranty of habitability is an example of a court-imposed policy not even addressing the correct problem!

Techniques for Answering the Question

- **TBA** — Think, Breathe, and Answer
- Listen closely to the question being asked
- Ask for clarification if you don't understand the question
- Volunteer if you know the answer instead of waiting to be cold-called
- Remember that the professor is a collaborator, not your adversary
- Be conversational and confident, not confrontational or arrogant

Chapter Four

Making a Formal Presentation
in a Class or on the Job

As you advance into upper-level courses in law school, you may enroll in smaller-group classes, such as seminars or clinics (where you represent real clients under the guidance of a professor). Very often in courses like these you will be required to lead one of the class discussions or present an oral report.

You may also encounter the challenge of making a formal verbal presentation during a summer job. Summer associates or newly minted lawyers are sometimes asked to make presentations to their colleagues, and this is the sort of assignment that you must accept. The request often arises in a guise of informality: "We'd like you to give a quick talk at the firm lunch about that case you're working on. Just bring us up to speed about what's been happening." Even if the norm at your law firm is to treat these occasions with a sort of cavalier informality—and even if more-senior lawyers at your workplace do a terrible job when they make these presentations themselves—you should take the assignment seriously. Realize that all eyes will be on you, and that your audience includes people who will decide whether to offer you a permanent job (if you are a summer associate) or whether to let you meet with clients or reward you with other plum assignments. This is a wonderful opportunity to bring yourself to the attention of people who can help make your career more enjoyable and successful. If you take the time to prepare and practice, you can shine.

For example, Alex found that his willingness to make a speech landed him a permanent job at the firm where he worked as a summer associate:

> After I wrote a research memorandum for an associate to prepare him for an upcoming presentation to the business department, the attorney offered me the chance to actually present the material myself. In essence, I was entrusted with the task of distilling a complex topic of contract law and its application in Maryland for attorneys who would, in turn, implement that knowledge in practice on a daily basis.

Alex knew that he could do the speech well because he had taken classes in law school that required him to make formal presentations, so he agreed to make the speech. After he spoke, several partners at the firm congratulated him on a job well done and expressed interest in working with him in the future. He also received an offer of permanent employment at a time when few firms were hiring. That shows you the power of verbal persuasion!

Here's what you need to know to deliver a memorable speech in a class or on the job.

Your Goals: *Ethos, Pathos* and *Logos*

As you craft a formal verbal presentation, keep in mind what you are trying to accomplish. You of course are trying to satisfy the requirements of the assignment — so, for example, if you have been asked to describe a series of cases to your seminar classmates, you should make sure that your talk covers all the cases. But you have objectives beyond this as well, like impressing your classmates or colleagues with your intelligence. Or demonstrating some skill — adroitness with a tricky legal situation, perhaps, or power as a public speaker. You want to keep things interesting, so that people will pay attention to you. And you want the audience to like you enough to approach you after the talk and ask you questions about it, or want to work with you in the future. That requires something more from you than simply slogging through the cases you have been assigned.

Believe it or not, these basic goals of oral persuasion have been guiding speakers for over 2,000 years, practically since people first began talking to one another. Aristotle offered a formulation for successful verbal presentation in his work *The Rhetoric*, which can be a helpful way to understand what you hope to achieve each time you approach the lectern. In order to be persuasive, a speaker must exhibit the following:

Ethos is the manifestation of good character. The audience needs to believe that you are a credible speaker — that you know what you're talking about, and that you will not unfairly slant the facts.

Pathos is the effective use of emotion. To be convincing, the audience needs to believe you care about your topic, and you must figure out how to make the audience care as well. But try to avoid overusing emotion. If the audience believes that you are overwhelmed with emotion — if, for example, you seem terrified or angry, or begin to cry — then your credibility (your ethos) is compromised.

Audiences also are persuaded by *logos*, or clear logic. Your goal is to make your reasoning comprehensible and reasonable.

If you can achieve the triple goals of ethos, pathos, and logos in your presentation, you are sure to impress. But how can you make this happen? With these goals in mind, we'll walk through the process of writing and rehearsing a spoken presentation.

Writing the Presentation

Find a Theme

A verbal presentation requires a different style of writing from the kind that you may have become accustomed to using when you wrote an essay in college, or when you write a legal memo or brief. Your audience needs to be able to grasp the heart of your message right away, without the luxury of being able to flip back and forth through your manuscript to re-read sections or look up words they don't understand. You certainly want all your writing to be crisp, clear, and attention-grabbing, but when you are writing a *verbal* presentation, these goals are even more critical.

Having a convincing theme—a pithy phrase or sentence that sums up the core of your message—can help sort out the structure of your talk and make your presentation clear to your audience. For example, imagine that your talk at the firm-wide lunch is about a lawsuit you have brought on behalf of a manufacturer of building supplies against a dozen insurance companies that issued it insurance policies over the years. You hope that the case will recover millions of dollars of insurance proceeds for your client, but right now you are mired in reviewing thousands of documents to see if they must be produced to opposing counsel. You could stand up and say, "I'm going to talk to you about our lawsuit against a bunch of insurance companies, and all the boxes of documents that we have been looking at this summer." If you do, your audience will be snoozing in no time.

A snappy theme can change this. Perhaps you start the speech instead like this:

> Imagine that you have been asked to represent a company that used to make building products that contained asbestos, back before anyone knew how dangerous asbestos is. Your client has been through the wringer— the business has been slapped with many lawsuits by shipyard workers who were hurt by asbestos, and the lawsuits have taken their toll. Your client, of course, bought insurance over the years that should cover it for losses like these, but the insurance companies are refusing to pay. So you've sued all 12 of the insurers, and the lawsuit is rolling forward. Now you're in discovery, and you've been served with requests for documents by all of them. You've met with the workers at your client's office who are likely to have the documents that you will need to produce, and you've amassed a team

of paralegals who will help you comb through the piles of papers. But just as you are about to start work, you get a call from your client's general counsel. The company is really suffering, and they've had to lay off hundreds of employees, including all the people who were going to get you those documents you need and answer the questions you have about them. Now what? I'm going to talk to you today about Coming Up with Plan B When Plan A is Laid Off, or the need for flexibility in litigation.

There's your theme—the need for flexibility in litigation—and now you know the point you want to hammer home. You should return to your theme at several points during the presentation (perhaps by telling a few stories about challenges in the document review and how you overcame those challenges by exhibiting flexibility), and also at the end ("So my take-home message is … think outside the box! It makes all the difference!"). Each time you repeat the theme, you'll want to say it loudly and with confidence to emphasize it. A theme is a way to engage the audience—the start of pathos. If you are confident about it, you will exhibit ethos as you speak of it because you will believe in it, which will make your listeners believe in it, too. And if you have found a theme that fairly distills the essence of your message, then your logos becomes clearer to your listeners as well.

Craft Your Structure

The listeners need to be able to hear the structure of your presentation in order to follow it. When you write something that's meant to be read rather than heard, the structure is made clear visually through chapter headings or big white spaces between sections. But when you have a verbal presentation, you need to make the structure clear through writing and delivery. If the audience cannot sense the structure—where one point ends and the next begins—then the whole speech feels like a lump and is much more difficult to understand or pay attention to. You cannot attain logos without a clear structure.

To achieve a clear structure, you must make choices about the points you will address. You cannot hope to tell your audience every single thing that you know about the topic. If you were chosen to speak, then presumably you know quite a lot and could rattle on for hours! Your goal is not to demonstrate the breadth of your knowledge, but instead to communicate with your audience a few well-chosen points in order to bring your central message home. The strongest speeches do not make 100 points; they make three or four, but they make them well. If you insist that you must make 100 points (or if your professor or supervisor insists that you must), then try to find ways to clump them into three or four sections that go together. For example, using our insurance lawsuit talk, perhaps you include three or four discrete scenarios that arose during the document review, and while each one could include multiple issues, using the scenarios will provide structure in the talk as you move from one event to another.

You can signal to your listeners that you are moving from one section to the next through what you say and how you say it. You might want to write an explicit road map into your speech: "To show you what I mean by flexibility, I'd like to share with you three stories about our representation of The Building Company this summer. The first story starts at the beginning of the summer, with that fateful telephone call informing us of the layoffs." After you've told that story, you return to the structure: "Thus ends our first story. Our second is a bit darker. It takes place a month later, at a warehouse in Ohio." You can also signal moments of transition in your speech by pausing as you move from section to section; by changing your location (perhaps taking a step to a different part of the stage); by bringing out a visual aid or advancing to a new PowerPoint slide; or by changing the tone of your delivery a bit (perhaps from something lighthearted to something more serious).

Structure is critical to make your speech understandable. If your structure is clear, your logos will be clearer, too.

Pay Special Attention to Your First and Last Paragraphs

The beginning and ending of any verbal presentation are particularly important because these are the moments that your audience is most likely to hear and remember. That beginning moment is when you make your first impression and when the audience's attention is the most keen. The ending is the final impression that you make on your listeners, and (if their minds have wandered a bit) is when they are likely to snap to attention again.

You can make the most of your beginning and your ending paragraphs by highlighting the theme of your talk in as vivid a way as you can. Think about how to grab the audience's attention with your first paragraph. Don't waste that first impression on needless wind-up; instead, jump right into the heart of whatever has made the topic interesting to you and will make it interesting to them. Learn the beginning of your speech by heart so you can deliver that first paragraph without having to read it from your notes. Crafting an introduction that you enjoy delivering can help a great deal with stage fright, and can make all the paragraphs that come after go much more smoothly.

Your ending should hearken back to the theme that you established in your first paragraph, but with some additional insight. You might think of the final paragraph as "theme plus"—the theme plus whatever action you hope your audience will take. Your speech will be more meaningful and memorable to your audience if you structure it around takeaways they can use. So back to our Building Company example—an appropriate ending for that speech might be something like:

> So that is the story of how our team is meeting the challenges of producing documents in the face of mass internal layoffs at the client corporation. It really boils down to three lessons: First, while you of course must keep in mind the needs of your client, the company, you will also want to be sensitive to the concerns of the people who work at the company to understand why they might not always act in a way that is in the client's best interests. Second, when the rest of the world is falling apart, you will do much better if you have a plan—and if that plan uses technology wisely. You'll see handouts in the back of the room with more information about the database programs I've described during this talk, which may be of use to you in your work. And third, even in the darkest of hours, you must keep your sense of humor (and your wits) about you. That's what can turn what at first appears to be a tedious task into an interesting and satisfying assignment.

Get Their Attention Back

You can expect that every three or four minutes, even the most attentive audience member's mind will wander from even the most skilled speaker's speech. As you design your presentation, think about ways to reengage the flagging attention of the audience at various points. You can do this in a number of ways. You can get people's attention back by emphasizing the structure—by saying, "I am now moving to the next argument," or by making a transition clear through your delivery by pausing, raising your volume, or gesturing. You could pull out a visual aid or advance to a new PowerPoint slide. You could pause to ask a question of the audience or ask for a show of hands ("How many of you have had this kind of experience?"). You could illustrate a point with an anecdote—people's ears always perk up if you have a story to tell. You could play a video or audio clip to add some variety to the presentation.

Use Clear Language

When you are making a verbal presentation, it's important to use language that everyone can understand. If you need to discuss a concept that experts would use jargon to explain, do your audience the kindness of defining the jargon for them or avoiding it altogether. In an environment like a law school class or a law firm, it's sometimes important to use a specific legal term, also known as a *term of art*, to show the experts in the room (like the professor) that you know it. But you can rest assured that there will be other intelligent people in the room who are not familiar with the term who are still very interested in following along with the presentation. Keep them in mind, and tell them what the term means. For example, as you make your Building Company presentation, you may want to show a "coverage chart" to illustrate which insurers have "indemnified" the company during "policy periods," and what their "coverage levels" are. Explain all those terms. ("This colorful thing is a coverage chart, which as you can see is a way of showing the insurance policies that The Building Company bought over the years, and the amount of money that they thought they would be able to recover under the terms of each policy.")

Verbal presentations must be clear in order to be meaningful. If a presentation is riddled with unfamiliar words, the speaker will have a much harder time connecting with the audience, who will either feel out of place because they cannot understand, or annoyed because they are forced to expend a lot of energy translating the big words. A speaker who is really focused on sharing an idea with his audience will use that audience's language, which will make him much more believable than one who seems to be showing off rather than genuinely trying to communicate. If you want to see a great example of this principle at work, listen to one of Franklin Delano Roosevelt's "fireside chats," which were a series of radio speeches given to the American people during the Great Depression. Roosevelt explained complex ideas about banking and currency so clearly that Will Rogers said that he took "such a dry subject as banking ... [and] made everyone understand it, even the bankers."[1] Roosevelt appeared to be making every effort to communicate with his audience on their terms; as a result, they trusted him and he was able to restore confidence in the banking system. Lawyers sometimes fall into the habit of peppering their sentences with jargon without even realizing they are doing it. This is a mistake if you hope to be understood and trusted. Your goal is to make complexity lucid and comprehensible.

Give Yourself Ample Rehearsal Time

Once you've decided on a possible theme, written a first draft of your first and last paragraphs, and figured out the points you would like to make in the

---

1. *Will Rogers' Daily Telegrams, Volume 4: The Roosevelt Years 1933–1935*, at 4 (James M. Smallwood & Steven K. Gragert eds., 1979).

middle, it's time to start practicing the presentation out loud. At this point your script is not finalized. You'll make adjustments as you rehearse. It's easy to identify overly complicated language when you rehearse out loud—those are the words that you trip over every time. You will be able to spot problems with your logic—those are the places where you consistently forget what paragraph comes next (which means that you should try rearranging those sections). You'll also be able to find the moments where you most connect with the material, and those will be the points at which you will want to engage the audience's emotions to achieve pathos.

When you practice, you must do it out loud. It's simply not the same exercise to silently read a script to yourself—you must try the words out and see how they feel in your mouth. If you come upon a section that feels awkward to you, then rewrite it. If there's a part that's hard to deliver, see if the language needs to be simplified or if a long sentence should be cut in half to make it easier to take a breath. You cannot find these problem spots if you've never tried the speech out loud before.

Rehearsing aloud also helps you really learn the text of your talk. If you hear your own familiar voice delivering the ideas, then you begin to memorize them, just as if you were learning the words to a new piece of music. Try rehearsing just before going to sleep at night, because then the ideas linger in your mind and often are ingrained when you wake up the next morning. The more you know what you plan to say, the more confident you will feel and, consequently, the stronger your credibility will appear. It's also easier to connect with your audience (pathos) if you can put down your script and look them in the eye while speaking.

Try rehearsing standing up if this is the sort of speech that should be delivered standing (as most formal presentations are), and practice exactly the sort of body language you plan to use during the speech. I first observed how critical this is when I began to run summer workshops to help faculty members improve their lecturing skills at the law school where I teach. Some professors paced back and forth like a lion in a cage while lecturing—a distracting habit. Very often, this type of speaker admitted to pacing in his office when practicing or even just while thinking aloud, and so it became second nature and a difficult habit to break. If you rehearse instead with confident body language, you will ingrain positive mannerisms that won't detract from your message.

Speaking on Short Notice

If you find yourself in the stressful situation of having to present a speech with little advance notice, spend the time that you have figuring out your theme and picking three good points to illustrate it. For example, imagine that you are working at the Department of the Treasury for the summer, and you are asked to explain a new regulation to a group of lawyers. Resist the temptation to simply read the long, boring regulation to your audience. Focus on theme and structure. The regulation has probably been enacted to address a prob-lem—that problem is your theme. It may have numerous subparts, so pick the three that your audience is most likely to encounter, and take the time to explain them. As for the rest of it, give them a handout with the entire regula-tion on it so they can read the parts you didn't talk about on their own.

Then prepare a quick one-page list of notes to help you deliver the talk. Make the notes bullet points rather than complete sentences so that you will not be tempted to simply read your remarks. Each bullet point should remind you of a point you want to make. This will help keep the talk conversational, and makes it more likely that you will reach for the kinds of words that you use in everyday life. Make a note of how you'll start and how you'll end. An easy be-ginning would be: "Here's the kind of problem that we see every day in our line of work," a description of the problem, and then a description of the regulation that will solve the problem. Your ending? Circle back to the beginning, and give them an action item: "So the next time you see one of these problems, reach for this regulation. It will help you."

Use the remaining time to practice the presentation out loud. If you don't have time to run through the whole speech, just practice the first and last paragraphs.

Delivery Matters

Your goal when you deliver any type of speech is to appear as confident and relaxed as possible, because this will make your audience trust you. If you seem nervous or ill-at-ease, your audience may think that you are uncomfortable with your message and will be less likely to believe you. To build that trust, practice sounding conversational—not like you are reading some prepared re-marks. This will make you seem more engaging and genuine to listeners, who have trouble sitting through dry or dull deliveries. You can see this in course evaluations of law school professors. Students call the professors who are stilted "dry" or "boring," but the teachers who can relax during their presentation yield comments like, "It was never difficult to pay attention to the entire 1.5 hours of this class every day."

Appearing natural and "doing what comes naturally" are not the same things, though. It can be intimidating to stand before an audience of severe-looking people and talk to them. Your natural impulse may be to run and hide! Don't. Instead, you can achieve a natural, confident delivery style by forcing yourself to speak up in public as much as possible so that you gain experience, practicing your remarks many times so that you really know what you want to say, writing a speech that you are comfortable with, and analyzing your delivery style so you can emphasize the things you do well and break any habits that might be detracting from your performance.

Distracting delivery habits tend to fall within some defined categories, so let's look at each one in turn.

What to Do with Your Feet

Start with your stance, which affects everything about your body language. If you stand tall, your voice will sound stronger, you will appear more confident, and people will be more likely to believe what you are saying. Conversely, if you shift your weight, stand awkwardly, or pace, an audience may be distracted or think that you are uncomfortable with your argument.

Every speaker needs to cultivate a "home base," or a stance that will let you be still and commanding for a long period of time. Try standing with your feet hip-width apart (essentially as wide as they would be if separated by your two fists next to one another — no wider), with your knees soft (not locked). Your shoulders should be rolled back but relaxed (not clenched up toward your ears). Your ears should be directly over your shoulders, not jutted out in front of them. Here's a way to get into this posture that can also be a good daily exercise to help you improve your physical presence:

- Place your feet hip-width apart, measuring the distance by putting your two fists between your feet.
- Stand up straight and reach up high, stretching up tall.
- Now flop over at the waist, letting your spine cascade forward. Your arms should be dangling, reaching towards the floor. Make sure your head is loose by nodding "yes" and "no."
- Take a few slow breaths as you stay bent over, feeling your back expand and contract with each breath. Let the breaths fill the small of your back, then the middle part of your spine, then your shoulder blades.
- Finally, roll up slowly, one vertebra at a time. Try to stack the vertebrae one on top of the other so that you will be standing with a straight spine. Your head will be the last thing to come up.
- Roll your shoulders back, lift your chin, let your arms dangle by your sides with your hands gently cupped, and make sure that your feet are

still about hip-width apart and your knees aren't locked. This is your "home base" stance.

Often, people do not give much thought to their "home base," and instead stand with their feet very close together—which looks tense and also makes it much harder to stay balanced, causing you to sway. Sometimes they know they sway and so adopt an overly wide stance in order to stay still—which looks odd and makes the audience think, "Why is he standing like he's ready for a shoot-out at the O.K. Corral?" Some people like to cross their feet, resulting in more swaying or very odd postures reminiscent of a ballet dancer. Some rock back on their heels; some bob up on their toes. All of these things distract your listeners. Avoid incessant pacing or a weaving motion at all costs.

While wandering or pacing as you speak is distracting, moving with a purpose can be a great way to add some power to your presentation. You may have seen great trial lawyers do this during a closing argument, for example. If you have the impulse to move as you speak, then do, but think about using changes in your position to make your structure more clear. For example, as you transition from one point to another, you might take a step or two to a new place on the stage. But then *stand still* once you have assumed your new position. If you move haphazardly or too frequently, you will hypnotize the audience and detract from your message.

If you want to incorporate walking but aren't sure how to do it, practice taking a couple of steps (and no more) each time you move from one point to another. For example, at our transition of, "Thus ends our first story. Our second is a bit darker. It takes place a month later, in Ohio," start to walk as you say, "Our second is a bit darker." Finish the walk and take your new spot on the stage by the time you say "Ohio." This can help make the progression to a new point clear. You could also pull out a visual aid, approach a chart to point out something in particular, or distribute a handout—all are great reasons to move. You may have seen trial lawyers use this technique, for example by approaching a witness with an exhibit during an examination. If you give yourself a reason to move during your presentation, you add visual interest and re-engage the audience's attention. If you decide to walk, then do it with confidence. No timid half-steps!

Be mindful of the personal space of the audience and also of what they are able to see. If you get too close to your audience (for example, in the context of a courtroom, if you were to lean against the jury box as you speak to the jury), you will make the audience uncomfortable. If you have moved in order to show the audience a visual aid, make sure that you are not blocking the visual aid with your body. Take care not to turn your back to the audience at any time, because this breaks your eye contact with them and also turns your voice away from them, making you more difficult to hear. If you suspect that your audience cannot see what you want them to see, ask them whether they would like to move. Lawyers in jury trials sometimes ask the jurors to give them a "thumbs up" if they can see/hear something. It's perfectly fine to talk to the audience and encourage them to stand up or come closer, or for you to adjust as needed, during the talk. They will be grateful that you are keeping their viewpoint in mind.

What to Do with Your Hands

In everyday conversation, people use their hands to communicate. You don't even have to think about it to do it well. Typically, you have some moments of stillness as you speak — it is the rare person who gesticulates constantly. But you also have some moments of motion. If you are speaking with your hands and arms completely frozen, the person you're talking to will likely ask you if something is wrong!

Similarly, in a verbal presentation you will appear more natural and confident if your delivery includes some motion and some moments of stillness. Many of my students find this to be one of the most difficult things to achieve at first, because if you are feeling self-conscious, your hands suddenly appear to be larger and clumsier than they really are. Very often, nervous speakers have the impulse either to hide their hands — thrusting them in pockets, or winding them up in crossed arms or a death-grip with one another — or else use them to gesture repetitively, which can drive an audience mad.

Just as you have done with your feet, you should find a resting place for your hands that permits you graceful moments of stillness, but that leaves your hands free and available for you to use when the impulse arises. One of the most powerful resting places for hands is called "actor's neutral." This is the position that your hands were in when you finished the spinal-roll exercise described in the preceding section. Your arms are simply dangling by your sides, and your hands are loosely cupped.

Now that you know about actor's neutral, start to look for it when you see a performance like a play or an opera. You are likely to see it everywhere. It is a very strong posture because it permits your voice to be rich and supported, and it encourages you to stand up straight. Plus, to an audience, it communicates nothing but confidence. Other favorite resting places that people adopt unthinkingly are not neutral at all. They communicate something: Holding one hand with the other says that you are uncomfortable; putting your hands in your pockets is sloppy and too casual; folding your arms across your chest indicates that you are unreceptive (or else that the air conditioning is on too high); and clasping your hands behind your back is a stiff, military posture. Hands in actor's neutral simply says, "I am confident."

But don't stay frozen in actor's neutral throughout your talk. Try to find some places to move your hands. It's natural to move your hands if you tell an anecdote to illustrate a point, or in a section of the talk that describes a scene. You can move your hands at the moments of pathos — those power moments when you are pleading your case or driving your theme home. If you are not a natural gesturer, try incorporating a visual aid into the presentation. That will give you a reason to use your hands. You can also try one rehearsal where you force yourself to remain perfectly still as you deliver your talk. Notice the places where that drove you crazy. Those are the moments where you should use your hands.

How can you tell if your hand gestures are repetitive? I don't recommend rehearsing in front of a mirror because this can make you self-conscious. If you watch yourself as you are speaking, it affects your performance and can lead to some odd results. Instead, video record a rehearsal. Then you can watch the footage to see if there are any problem areas you would like to smooth out. It can also be extremely helpful to have a more experienced mentor watch you rehearse to give you suggestions.

Sometimes repetitive hand gestures happen because your resting place is mid-torso rather than arms down at your sides — this can lead to truncated hand gestures that begin to look repetitive. If that's the problem, try using actor's neutral until it becomes second nature. Sometimes the problem can be fixed when you really know your script well and can firmly concentrate on simply communicating your message, rather than feeling anxious about what word comes next. But the best magic bullet is rehearsal and repetition. Repetitive hand gestures are often a habit, so you have to give yourself plenty of rehearsal time in order to break bad habits and acquire better ones.

Use Your Best Voice

If you want your logos to be clear, and if you want to achieve ethos and pathos, then you have to speak up. If your audience cannot hear you, it's as if you never made a presentation at all.

A good, strong volume is essential to a successful presentation, and affects your ethos as well. The speaker who mumbles or whispers appears unsure of his own authority. To make certain that your volume is strong, look audience members in the eye and speak to the person sitting in the back row. Practice that home-base stance so that you are using good posture — this helps keep your voice powerful. If you are in the habit of speaking softly, conduct at least three rehearsals in which you concentrate on raising your volume to a level your elderly grandmother could hear. It can be helpful to practice over white noise (which, believe it or not, you can find on the Internet or download as an iPhone app), and then keep that same volume when the white noise has been turned off.

Watch for verbal tics. Many people pepper their speeches with filler sounds, such as "um," "like," "you know," or "okay." Words are precious. Stay away from garbage words and instead use the ones that mean something. To break the filler-sound habit, make sure you know your speech well. It can be helpful to videotape a rehearsal or two and notice where the "ums" creep in. That's a section you should practice aloud again several times. The better you know your talk, the less likely you are to reach for a filler word. If you find that a particular sentence or word of your speech escapes you, it's stronger and less noticeable simply to pause rather than to fill the space with an "um." Also, don't worry too much about getting the script exactly right. Remember that the audience doesn't have a copy of your script. They won't know if you jumbled a word here or there, so long as you don't let on with a filler sound.

Another verbal tic that can undercut your ethos is the habit of ending every sentence with an upward inflection, as if the statement were a question. If you make your declarative statements into questions, you seem to question your own message and your right to be speaking to the audience in the first place. It can be helpful to rehearse with a friend or mentor to break this habit. Tell this person to tap the table, stomp on the floor, or whack you with a rolled-up magazine every time you sound as if you are asking a question when you don't mean to. That habit will soon become a thing of the past.

Voices are more interesting to listen to if the speaker uses many notes, rather than speaking in a monotone or getting stuck at a high pitch. Pay attention to whether your voice box locks up when the adrenaline hits (as it does for many people), which can often be the cause of being stuck at an unnatural or monotone pitch. To add more life to your voice, try making your speech as interesting as it would be if you were telling a group of Girl Scouts gathered around a camp fire a ghost story, and they can't see you well. Or try another rehearsal in which you imagine that your speech is being broadcast over the radio and you only have your voice to engage people. This will help you find ways to reach for a variety of notes as you speak.

Try a vocal warm-up before making a speech. It can help relax and center you, and lets you take control of that adrenaline so you have only enough to give you a nice burst of energy, but not so much that you feel panicked. Here's a quick vocal warm-up that you can spend 10 minutes on each time you speak in public:

Vocal Warm-Ups

- Stretch and shake out your hands, arms, legs, and feet.
- Roll your shoulders back. Pull them up towards your ears and then let them drop.
- Do head rolls.
- Blow "raspberries," which is blowing air through your loosely closed lips, making a "brrr" noise. Now add sound. Go low to high, high to low.
- Massage and then relax your jaw.
- Stretch as high as you can. Then flop over, releasing all the air in your body.
- Hum as you hang from the waist. Feel the hum in your face, chest, back. If you've got a cold, spend some time on this exercise — it can help you sound less congested.
- Roll up slowly. Try to stack the vertebrae one on top of the other.
- Roll your shoulders back. Stand up straight.
- Take a deep breath, letting your arms float up as you inhale so that they are perpendicular to your sides. Now slowly exhale, letting the arms float down. Try to make the exhale last as long as you can. Repeat.
- Read and repeat the following sentence aloud, adding a phrase each time (demarcated by the "/"), slowly building up to the point where you can deliver it all in one breath:

  > I am now working/ on an important exercise/ for breath support and breath control/ and my aim is to control the breath easily/ without strain or tension of any kind/ to the end of this long, long sentence/ and still have enough breath left/ to sigh out like this: / ha.

- Try tongue-twisters. Each of the following phrases features different difficult consonant combinations. Start slow, over-articulating, and then increase your speed.

  Red leather, yellow leather

  Good blood, bad blood

  She sells sea shells by the seashore

  Teaching ghosts to sing

  The big, black-backed bumblebee

  Mommy made me mash my M&Ms

  Unique New York

  The tip of the tongue, the teeth, and the lips

Make Eye Contact

Looking people in the eye is an easy way to establish yourself as a credible speaker. When you look someone in the eye as you speak to them, you appear relaxed and confident about what you are saying. It's also easier to connect with that person and to notice that the listener has smiled at your joke or is nodding in agreement with the point you have made. Public speaking becomes much more fun when you pay attention to your audience and realize that they are listening to you!

Sometimes speakers stare fixedly at the floor or at the ceiling, above the audience's head, or at their notes. You may notice that audiences become restless when this happens because there is no connection between the speaker and the listener, and so the presentation feels lifeless. It can be helpful to video record your rehearsal to see whether you habitually avoid eye contact, and if you do, to practice looking at your audience. Start by delivering a few sentences of your speech while looking at people in a section of the room, and then look at the next section of the room, and so on. Think to yourself that you are trying to give an idea to each audience member, and you have to look at them to accomplish this. If you really have trouble with eye contact, ask five or six tolerant friends to serve as an audience while you rehearse. Start with your first paragraph, and deliver it while shaking hands with the first audience member. Then move to your next paragraph, and shake hands with the next audience member as you say it. Continue down the row. Once you've finished the exercise, do the speech again without shaking hands, but try to keep that same feeling of connection with the audience. Now, obviously, during a real presentation you won't be glad-handing with your listeners, but if you look them in the eye, you can bring them into the speech in the same way that you bring someone into a conversation by shaking hands.

Make an effort to include the entire room as you speak. You'll find that most audiences include "friendly faces" scattered here and there—look at those people especially. If someone in the audience looks unfriendly, ignore that person and assume that it has nothing to do with you. (I have learned this from years of teaching—if a student whispers to another student, I immediately think it is a negative comment about me. It rarely is—students are much less interested in my performance than they are in their own lives.) If many people in the audience look unfriendly, or bored, or confused, then perhaps they are responding to something in your talk. In that case you might want to adjust in response to the valuable feedback you are receiving. For example, you could say, "I can see that I've confused some of you. Let's pause here for some questions. What can I clarify?" Or you could say, "We've been going for a while now. This would be a good time for a quick water break, and we'll resume the talk in five minutes."

Think About Rhythm: Pausing and Pace

A truly wonderful speaker plays with the rhythms of language to make it sing. If you listen to Dr. Martin Luther King Jr. deliver his famous "I Have a Dream" speech, you can hear how the starts and stops in King's delivery pack an emotional wallop.

You needn't copy Dr. King if that's not your style, but it's important to pay attention to the rhythms of your speech to make sure you aren't stuck at a single speed. If you're speed-speaking, for example, the audience won't be able to understand you. You may know you are a speed-speaker because people in your everyday life (like your mother) have complained about it in the past, or maybe you only do it when nerves strike during a formal presentation. Realize that a speed that seems natural to you may still be too fast for the audience because they are hearing the material for the first time. If you are a speed-speaker, write "Slow down!" at the top of every page of your notes and highlight it. Pay attention to your breath—if you feel short of breath, then you are probably rattling along too quickly. Rehearsal can also help break the speed-speaking habit.

Whether or not you speak too quickly, think of your speech like a piece of music and find places to go more slowly, or to pause for a moment. Pauses generally should be about a half-second longer than what feels natural, because speakers usually underestimate the length of their pauses. Try pausing as you finish one point and begin the next, so that the audience can change gears with you. Try slowing down a particularly important point to emphasize its significance, or speeding up a section of a speech that involves action, to enhance the drama. When you listen to speeches in plays or movies, or by truly fine politicians speaking to a crowd, analyze the rhythms of the speech—you may find that the speaker's rhythm was what enabled him to achieve pathos. Once you begin to notice how it's done, it becomes fun to play with pace and pausing in speeches of your own.

Overcoming Fear of Public Speaking

You've written the perfect script—it's organized, interesting, and engaging. You've practiced it over and over again until you can say it in your sleep. You've prepared a few notes to carry with you, but you don't expect that you will need them. On the day of the speech, it hits you. You stand up to deliver your presentation, and look out on a group of attorneys—all much older than you, all with much more impressive credentials, and all of them staring right at you. Even students who are terrific at interviews or cold calls might experience jitters in a situation like this one. In fact, if you're not a little nervous, you probably don't care enough about what you're doing.

But it's important to remember that people of all ages and professions experience fear of public speaking—and lawyers are no exception. (In fact, I always feel a twinge of nervousness on my first day of class as I begin my first lecture, and I've been lecturing for years.) The first way to begin overcoming these butterflies is to breathe. It sounds simple enough, but you would be amazed at how easy it is to start talking quickly and forget to breathe during a speech.

When you forget to breathe, you'll find that you begin to trail off at the ends of sentences because you've run out of air. It becomes more difficult to enunciate your words clearly. Your voice might begin to shake. In other words, you will sound and feel even more nervous because your voice is doing all the things that a nervous person's voice does. If you make sure to breathe, you will be more physically comfortable when you speak. You will sound more confident — even if you are secretly terrified.

It can also help to adjust the way that you are thinking about your speech. Don't see your audience as a group of skeptics, waiting to sneer the second you mess up. Most people aren't like that at all. In fact, most audience members are silently rooting for you because they don't like public speaking much themselves and will be happy to applaud you for giving it a try. Your audience is there to learn something from you, so don't focus on trying to impress them. Focus instead on giving them something to take away from your speech. What do you want them to learn and remember?

It can also help to recall why you care about the topic. In an ideal world, the topic of your speech is something that engages you, and you will be able to convey that interest to the audience. If you did not choose the subject of the speech — if a partner asks you to present on some legal issue, for instance — tap into the aspects of the topic that you can convey with enthusiasm. If you focus on presenting the content of your speech in a way that is engaging and helpful, you will be worried about things that matter — keeping the audience's attention, speaking clearly, and providing the audience with information that they can use at a later date. With all of that in your mind, you won't have time to worry about whether you sound funny or are smart enough to do the job.

Perhaps the most important key to giving a successful speech is knowing that you are going to give a successful speech. It sounds circular because it is. Confidence is not a magic pill you can swallow 10 minutes before your speech (although that would be nice). Confidence in public speaking is an active process by which you reaffirm to yourself that you are up to the challenge of giving a great presentation — and you are. In the minutes before you stand up to speak, you might notice your stomach doing somersaults or find that a million new worries are entering your mind. This is not at all unusual, and happens to even the most experienced public speakers. Rather than giving into this feeling, take advantage of it. It's adrenaline coursing through your body, and you can use those jitters to give your speech a little extra energy to make it pop. Breathe deeply and think about the main message of your speech. If you have written an excellent speech and practiced it repeatedly, you should know that you are well prepared and that the only thing you have to fear is fear itself. And if you forget every line of your script, then think about that central theme and explain it to the audience. Don't worry if it's not letter-perfect—they'll never realize it if you don't let them. Channel those nerves into excitement and positive energy, and you will find the confidence and passion to make your speech great.

Final Thoughts

Public speaking becomes easier the more you do it. So give yourself plenty of time to practice, and cajole yourself to speak up as much as you can. If you follow the ideas outlined in this chapter, you'll find that your presentation will be easier for the audience to understand and more fun for you to deliver.

Chapter Five

First-Year Moot Court and Beyond

Many law schools require first-year students to take a year-long legal research and writing class. The first semester of this class arms you with the fundamentals of how to conduct basic legal research and write a legal memo, which you will need to know for your first job. The second semester typically revolves around an appellate advocacy exercise requiring you to write an appellate brief and make an oral argument before a mock court of appeals. The judges on the court might include a real judge, a graduate or two from your law school who are now practicing attorneys, or perhaps an upper-level student or your legal research and writing professor. Even though this is a simulated appellate argument, the experience can be as daunting as the real thing because it's your first time making an argument in a court. This chapter will help you prepare for that experience, as well as for moot court activities that you might engage in during upper-level classes or as an extracurricular activity.

What Is an Oral Argument?

The typical exercise in a first-year legal research and writing class asks you to imagine that you are an appellate attorney. You are usually given a *record* of what has happened in the case so far. This might include the trial court's decision on the legal issue you're now being asked to appeal, and perhaps briefs from the parties that were submitted at the trial phase. It could also include some sort of evidentiary record, such as transcripts of what the witnesses said at trial. Typically, your case will raise two issues; you are expected to address one, and your assigned partner will address the other.

In this exercise, students spend most of their time researching and writing an appellate brief arguing for their side of the issue. Your legal research and writing professor will tell you the rules of your court, such as how long the brief must be, how it should be formatted, and when it's due. Pay attention to those rules because your instructor is likely to enforce them exactly, just as a real court would. After you submit your brief, you will then be expected to argue your position aloud before a panel acting the part of judges. This is the oral argument.

The process of writing the brief is exhausting, and as a result, many law students don't prepare properly for the oral argument that follows. This is a mistake. It can be demoralizing to appear before a panel of judges, even pretend judges, and realize you don't know what to say. Ill-prepared students emerge from the experience shaken and battered; some of them make the decision then and there not to become litigators, when in fact they might, with practice, develop the skills needed to be brilliant trial or appellate attorneys. With a little preparation, your oral argument will be just fine — or even a transformational experience that reveals inner resources you didn't realize you have.

Before the Oral Argument

How to Prepare

The bulk of your oral argument will involve answering the judges' questions. Even though their questions guide the argument, you can influence the shape of the discussion. Your goals are to get the court to pay attention to, and agree with, your strongest arguments, and to explain your ideas in a way that the court can understand. Here's how to prepare.

Making an oral argument is not the same thing as simply standing up and reading your brief out loud. When you write a brief, you can cram it full of information, expecting that the judge may take the time to parse every footnote. Oral argument should be less about that minutia, and more about the big picture. Think of it as an opportunity to focus the judges on your most important points. Keep in mind that you typically are allotted 15 minutes to argue, and that those 15 minutes are shared with two or three judges. They will probably interrupt you midway through an answer, take information out of order, cut each other off, and very rarely permit you to finish an overly drawn-out thought. That means you should be selective about what to focus on at oral argument, both in terms of the number of points you will make, and in terms of their quality.

What is the heart of your argument, the most important point that you must establish in order to win? If you have this clearly in mind, then you'll know what to emphasize in your answers. Take the time to figure out what your core position is so that you can come back to it again and again during your argument. Don't get distracted by minor points that, if decided against you, won't change the outcome of your case. The more points you decide to address, the less time you will be able to spend on each, so narrow it down.

Your core position should be so clear to you that you can summarize it in a single, lucid sentence. Take, for example, the U.S. Supreme Court case *Barnhart v. Peabody Coal Co.,*[1] which involved a statute stating that the commissioner of Social Security "shall, before October 1, 1993," take a particular action. John Roberts, then an attorney representing Peabody Coal and later chief justice of the Supreme Court, opened his argument like this: "The petitioners' position is that when Congress said '*shall before* October 1st, 1993,' it meant *may before or after* October 1st, 1993."[2] By re-framing his opponent's position into a single sentence that sounded preposterous, Roberts was able to cut to the heart of his argument—that the text of the statute clearly says that the commissioner must act before October 1, 1993. (Peabody Coal lost the case, but Roberts's opening salvo remains effective, nevertheless.)

Determine whether the proposition for which you are arguing is broad or narrow so you can explain its limits to the court. A question testing those limits, or trying to extrapolate your proposition into a hypothetical future, is the most common type of question in an appellate argument. You should spend the bulk of your time practicing articulating those limits and consequences. For example, in the Supreme Court case *Morse v. Frederick,*[3] a high school student was suspended for displaying a poster that read "BONG HiTS 4 JESUS." Rather than framing this as a general free speech case, Kenneth Starr, arguing for the government, began his argument by stating, "Mr. Chief Justice, and may it please the Court: Illegal drugs and the glorification of the drug culture are profoundly serious problems for our nation." He went on to argue that the case only concerned speech about drugs and illegal substances—a much narrower focus with many fewer consequences, and one that the Court ultimately accepted.[4]

---

1. 537 U.S. 149 (2003).

2. You can listen to this part of the oral argument at 29:46, *Barnhart v. Peabody Coal Co.*, 537 U.S. 149 (No. 08-205), *available at* http://www.oyez.org/cases/2000-2009/2002/2002_01_705/argument.

3. 551 U.S 393 (2007).

4. You can hear this part of the oral argument at 9:05, *Morse v. Frederick*, 551 U.S 393 (No. 06-278), *available at* http://www.oyez.org/cases/2000-2009/2006/2006_06_278/argument.

Preparing for the Oral Argument

- Think "big picture"
- Focus the judges on your most important points
- Summarize your core position in a single sentence
- Anticipate questions the judges will ask
- "Moot" with a partner before the actual argument
- Prepare no more than two pages of notes to have in front of you at the lectern

---

The Importance of Practicing

To verbalize an idea confidently, you have to fully understand it. So practice—aloud—answering the questions that you think you will be asked. Trying to explain your answers out loud lets you find those places where your understanding is weak. Then you will be able to stop and think about your answer more deeply in order to make it better. An answer that looks perfectly fine in writing may feel awkward when you speak it, which lets you know you need to make adjustments.

Appellate advocates typically "moot" their arguments multiple times in advance to identify potential questions and practice articulating their answers. You and your moot court partner should plan to moot one another before the actual event to get comfortable discussing the concepts in the case.

You can anticipate many of the questions that the judges will ask. Try getting a bunch of index cards and writing a question on one side of a card and the answer on the other. Then shuffle the cards and practice your answers aloud, so that you feel confident you can take them in any order.

Kent, a third-year law student, describes how he prepared for his first-year oral argument, using techniques that he learned from his high school years:

> I made an outline of the arguments that I wanted to make and made sure that I had the broad points memorized, so that if I got asked questions I could get back to my broad points. I also made a list of all the cases that were cited in either brief and made sure I knew their holdings. I learned it well enough so that I had it memorized. In singing competitions, they tell you that until you can do it in the practice room 10 times perfectly by yourself, you're not going to be able to do it in front of people. I keep that in mind and make sure to prepare to a level higher than what I need to be able to do it on my own. So I would practice out loud to myself at home.
>
> When I was in high school I was in this competition called Bible Quiz, where you memorize books of the bible and [answer trivia about it]. It's a speed competition and so they'll ask questions and you buzz in as soon as you can answer the question. You have 30 seconds to answer, but the

answer could be as long as seven or eight verses, so you have to say them very, very fast. And if you don't anticipate what's going to be asked of you, and if you haven't practiced going through the answers fast enough, there's just no way that you're going to be able to do it in the time that they give you. And so, the only way that you can win is to anticipate and to practice out loud ahead of time. So I just applied those things to the oral argument and also to exams.

I think that strategy helped me win the award for best oral argument in my section.

At the Oral Argument

What to Expect on the Big Day

The oral argument for your case will probably be scheduled to last about an hour — 15 minutes for you to talk to the judges about your issue, 15 minutes for your partner to discuss his issue, and 15 minutes apiece for the students arguing the other side. Your legal research and writing professor will tell you the time limits in advance, and you can expect that they will be strictly enforced. The instructor may assign a student to act as the clerk of court, perhaps arming that student with signs indicating how much time you have left. When your time is finished, you are expected to stop talking.

Usually the courtroom is set up so the students representing the appellants (the side bringing the appeal) sit to the left as they face the judges, while the appellees (the side defending the decision of the lower court) are to the right. Wear a suit for your oral argument, and be there at least 15 minutes before the argument begins. You may sit prior to the proceedings, but stand when the clerk of court calls, "All rise!" The judges (typically, there will be two or three) will then enter the room and take their seats. You can sit again when the chief judge directs you to.

The chief judge then will usually say something like, "In the matter of *Smith v. Jones*, counsel for the appellants, you may proceed." That's the cue for the student arguing the first issue for the appellant to stand at the lectern.

What to Bring to the Lectern

You may see skilled appellate attorneys approach the lectern without any notes in their hands, but this is only for the very experienced (and not for the faint of heart). More typically, an advocate will bring something to the lectern to assist them in their arguments.

One helpful plan is to create no more than two sheets of notes in which you outline the key things that you want to say to the court (including citations to cases or pages within the record), or answers to likely questions. Take these two sheets of paper and staple them to the inside of a manila folder, one page per side. You can then take that folder to the lectern, open it, and see all your notes at a glance without having to turn pages. You could also have a three-ring binder with you with the record in it, with tabs to help you find the different pieces of the record quickly if needed. If all goes well, you will be able to rely exclusively on your manila folder, and will not have to open your binder at all, but it's comforting to know that if a judge asks you an unexpected question about the exact language of the lower court opinion or a piece of testimony, you'll be able to answer it. Some advocates bring their entire brief in outline form. This is a mistake — it can rattle you to have to turn pages frantically looking for some bit of information you cannot find. Instead, spend time creating the manila folder, and buttress it with notes about where you could find the original material in your binder if you have to.

Beginning the Argument

Some moot courts expect you to start with a recitation of the facts, which is also probably the first section you wrote in your legal brief. In real life, an appellate advocate rarely recites the facts because the judges are familiar with the briefs and are armed with *bench memos* (memos written by their law clerks) summarizing the facts. An appellate advocate would not want to waste any of his precious 15 minutes reciting facts; she would want to leap right to the central point of her legal argument. However, the reality of moot court is that the judges are lawyers who are volunteering their time; they may not have read the materials thoroughly. So the first of the two students arguing on behalf of the appellees should prepare a very short summary of the facts, making sure to emphasize the ones that are most helpful to her position. If you are the first student to speak, ask the court, "Would Your Honors like me to begin with a recitation of the facts of the case?" If the judges say no, you should plunge right into what you want the court to do.

During most moot court arguments, you will get about 30 seconds before the first judge interrupts with a question. Make those 30 seconds count. Start with a statement that outlines the shape of your argument: "Your Honors, there are three reasons that this court should affirm the lower court's decision. First, this outcome would be consistent with the plain meaning of the statute. Second, this is the most financially optimal outcome; an opposite result will require significant expenditures of government money in the future. And third, equity demands this result." Then you should explain your first assertion. Very often, judges will take note of what you've said and may even help you get through all the topics you outlined by saying something like, "Counsel, were you ever able to reach that third point you wanted to make?" Prioritize so that you make the most important point first. Advancing a weaker argument first erodes your credibility, and may mean that you never even get to the strongest argument.

Answering Questions During Argument

Advocating before a panel of judges is usually not the time to make a speech—it's more of a question-and-answer session. Look at the questions as a welcome event. The judges aren't trying to trip you up or make you appear stupid. If the questions sound aggressive, it could be that the panelists are arguing with one another or are simply frustrated as they work through a knotty legal problem. Don't spend time thinking that the judge is asking questions to make you feel bad. Instead, focus on the substance of the question itself and try to answer it as best you can.

Circle back to the heart of your case if you get a question that lets you highlight it. You could signal the importance of your central message by saying something like, "Your Honor, I think that goes right to the heart of this case." If you do that, the judge likely will really pay attention to what you say next.

Listen carefully and answer the question the judge has asked you, not the one you wish he'd asked. It's frustrating to a judge to ask a question and have the advocate respond, "I'm getting to that," or to duck the question. If the judge has asked something, it's because he's trying to work it out and wants to know what you think.

Be brief with your answers, because the judges will often interrupt you. You can frontload your answer with a short version ("Yes, and here's why"), because another judge might jump in before you can offer your full explanation. Simple answers are easier to deliver and less likely to be interrupted.

You should know what precedent exists in your jurisdiction, and whether the authority you are citing is binding or not, as discussed in Chapter Two. Don't, under any circumstances, mislead the court about the law. Don't say something like "it is well settled" or "all courts agree" if this is simply not the case. The judges will want to know what other decisions from their jurisdiction arguably apply, what the court controlling them has said, and what courts in other jurisdictions have said. You should be absolutely clear about which court said what, and what the precedential value of each decision is. Prepare notes listing all of this information so you can answer the inevitable questions about it.

Respond with full candor. Don't ever try to pretend away the obvious strength of the other side or the apparent weakness of your case. Deal with it head on. If you don't know the answer, say so, and offer to provide the court with a supplemental letter pointing them to the section of the record that answers their question. There probably won't be a mechanism in place for you to actually submit a supplemental letter as part of the classroom exercise, but this is how you might respond in real life. In real appellate arguments, lawyers arguing for the government may be asked what the government's position is about a particular proposition. If you are unsure what the official position should be, make this clear in your answer while doing your best to answer the question. You might say something like, "I am not certain of the government's position on this matter, but my understanding is that ___." You can then submit a letter to the court after the argument correcting the position if you got it wrong.

When hypotheticals differ substantially from the facts of your case, be wary of broadening your argument to fit a set of circumstances that are not central to your argument. Take, for example, *Citizens United v. Federal Election Commission*,[5] a landmark Supreme Court decision on campaign finance law. The case involved *Hillary: The Movie*, a documentary attacking Hillary Rodham Clinton, which the government argued could not be broadcast within 30 days of a primary because it was a broadcast advertisement mentioning a candidate. The attorney representing the government made the mistake of accepting a hypothetical by Justice Samuel Alito, in which he asked whether the government could ban the publication of a book that included an endorsement of a candidate for public office. Although the case could have been limited to deciding whether the infomercial at issue was similar to the political advertisements restricted by the statute, the government's attorney stated that the government could also prohibit books that feature campaign messages, opening a Pandora's box of First Amendment issues.[6] In the rehearing of the case, the government (now represented by Elena Kagan, who was later appointed to the Supreme Court) claimed that the statute did not, in fact, apply to books: "The Government's answer has changed, Justice Ginsburg."[7] But the damage had already been done, and the law was ultimately struck down on First Amendment grounds in an opinion that imagined a scenario in which a nonprofit group published a book advocating a position.[8] This is an important lesson for oral argument: Beware of the hypothetical that wanders beyond the limits of your position.

---

5. 558 U.S. 50 (2010).

6. Oral Argument at 32:20, *Citizens United v. Federal Election Commission*, 552 U.S 1240 (No. 08-205), *available at* http://www.oyez.org/cases/2000-2009/2008/2008_08_205/argument.

7. You can hear the reargument of *Citizens United v. Federal Election Commission*, 558 U.S 50 (No. 08-205), at http://www.oyez.org/cases/2000-2009/2008/2008_08_205/argument.

8. 130 S. Ct. at 897.

If a judge asks a two-part question, you might only be able to answer the first part before the subject changes. Or perhaps you start to answer a question when another judge interrupts. As the judges quiz you, make a quick note of the questions so you can remember to go back to complete your answer if you need to. The judge who asked the original question will appreciate it.

Finally, if there is a lull in the questioning, take charge. Move on to your next important point. Go back to your core position, bolstering it in a different way. Or go back and complete an answer to any hanging questions. If you've made all the points you wanted to make and the judges don't seem to have more questions, then sit down. Judges appreciate brevity.

What to Say During the Oral Argument

- Highlight your central message when possible
- Answer the question asked, not the question you wish they'd asked
- Be brief with your answers
- Never mislead the judges
- Confront the weaknesses in your case head-on
- Take charge if there is a lull in questioning

Using the Right Language

When you answer a question, reach for straightforward language rather than peppering your answer with legalese or other jargon. It's easier to understand a plain-language answer (and also much easier to say). Listen to some appellate arguments on the website www.oyez.com, which contains both briefs and audio recordings of oral arguments before the U.S. Supreme Court. Compare the oral argument to the brief filed in whatever case you are listening to and you'll see that the language is markedly different. The oral argument is likely to have simpler language.

Make your argument vivid. Drive your point home by connecting it to a real-world example, or use a well-chosen metaphor. It's extremely unlikely that an ideal metaphor or example will come to you at the lectern, so take the time to craft one in advance.

The oral argument in *Rosenberger v. University of Virginia*[9] provides a terrific example of how to use dramatic language to drive a point home. The case involved a student-run religious magazine called *Wide Awake*, which successfully

---

9. 515 U.S. 819 (1995).

sued the University of Virginia for refusing to fund it. The attorney for the university made a key point stand out by using repetition:

> Justice O'Connor, very early you asked me a question that I'd like to get to. I think it's the heart of the case.... [The petitioner's main] claim is that the university's guidelines are guilty of antireligious viewpoint discrimination. That is not true. The university funds, not opinions or viewpoints, but activities. The university does not fund *religious* activities. The university does not fund *antireligious* activities. If there were a journal of anti-religion, if there were a journal devoted primarily to denying the existence of a deity, we would not fund it. It would not be eligible for funding. And it would not be eligible on precisely the ground that *Wide Awake* is not eligible. If there were an anti-Christian newsletter, devoted primarily to denying the tenets of Christianity, we would not fund it. It would not be eligible for funding. And it would not be eligible for funding on precisely the ground that *Wide Awake* is not eligible for funding.

Notice how he first highlighted what he was going to say by flagging it as "the heart of the case." He did this during a lull in the questioning, which means that he took charge of the direction of the conversation rather than waiting passively for the topic to come up. He connected his statement to something Justice Sandra Day O'Connor had asked, which means that he was keeping track of the questions and doubled back to complete an answer that he had not been able to finish at first. By signaling that it was O'Connor's question, he certainly grabbed her attention, as well as the attention of any of her allies on the Court. And then he gave two examples to illustrate his point: a journal of anti-religion, and a journal opposed to Christianity. He used a great rhythm to make sure that the point sank in ("We would not fund it. It would not be eligible for funding. And it would not be eligible on precisely the ground that *Wide Awake* is not eligible.").

What to Say During the Oral Argument: Using the Right Language

- Use simple, straightforward language
- Make your argument vivid with real-world examples and metaphors
- Highlight important points, perhaps by flagging them as "the heart of the case"

Striking the Right Tone

A final caution about oral argument—there should be very little "arguing" involved. Do not bicker with the judges; instead, answer their questions. Don't quibble with opposing counsel or speak disparagingly of him or his case. Instead, address his best points fully and fairly, with a reasonable and confident tone. Too many lawyers turn every argument into an opportunity for bloodshed, which is tedious and off-putting to the judges deciding the matter. An aggressive tone doesn't improve your chances of winning, but it might make the judges more likely to challenge you.

Chapter Six

Trial Practice Classes and
Mock Trial Teams

Many of us first imagine becoming lawyers after watching a movie or TV show like *To Kill a Mockingbird* or *Law & Order*—dramas that make a courtroom look like a pretty inspiring place. During law school, you'll learn about many areas of practice that never require you to set foot in a courtroom, but even if you choose to specialize in a non-litigation field, you may still find yourself before a jury one day on behalf of a pro bono client. Courtroom advocacy can be tremendously exciting, and if you have any interest at all in the subject, don't miss the opportunity to take a trial practice class or perhaps even participate on a mock trial team. These experiences provide fundamental training for would-be litigators as well as other types of lawyers because they hone your ability to think on your feet and speak in public.

It's common for law students to feel daunted by this kind of public speaking at first. One student describes his experience this way:

> When I first started mock trial, I was terrified of public speaking—so terrified, in fact, that I seriously considered quitting. Every time I got up to speak, I started shaking. I was convinced that the more experienced team members were just better than I was, and there was nothing I could do about it.
>
> But I didn't want to let my team down in competition, so I decided that I would need to do some serious preparation if I was going to keep up. I scripted every question, practiced my opening statement over and over again until I was sick of it, and made note cards [listing] the objections I was likely to get.
>
> After my first competition, it all started to click. I got better at handling unexpected objections, and people started telling me that I was a "talented" public speaker (although I had no idea where this "talent" came from, since I had been a terrible public speaker just months earlier). It

occurred to me then that trial advocacy—and public speaking generally—is much more of a skill than a talent.

Today, mock trial is still a huge part of my life, and it continues to be
the most enjoyable activity I do. I coach an undergraduate mock trial
team and captained a team that finished third in the country. What I've
found most striking about coaching mock trial is how much other people's
experiences seem to mirror my own. Mock trial can be really
overwhelming at first. But after just a few weeks of practice (or a few
days, in some cases), almost everyone finds it immensely enjoyable. There
is no feeling in the world like sitting down after delivering a devastating
closing argument, or backing a witness into a corner with your cross-
examination, or winning an objection after making a creative argument
the other side hadn't anticipated.

The student also discovered that the skills he learned in mock trial helped him
elsewhere:

When I go into a job interview, I develop a theme, just like I would
for a closing argument, and can move back and forth between the more
scripted responses that I have anticipated to the ones that I have to develop
on the spot.

Mock trial often requires you to read, write, think, and speak within a
matter of moments. As a result, I've noticed I have a much easier time
multitasking on cold calls, since I can read my notes on the case, listen to
the professor, and think of a response at the same time.

Mock trial has helped my writing, too. I'm used to thinking in terms
of short, powerful sentences that are clear and persuasive, which is what
good lawyering is about. If you can write clearly enough for someone to
understand in an oral presentation, then your writing will be even clearer
when it's written down. The tangible skills that mock trial teaches are in-
dispensable to all kinds of legal work, and I don't know any way of learning those skills that would be more fun than mock trial.

What a Trial Looks Like

Before jumping into the finer points of courtroom advocacy, let's look at
the big picture of how trials work. Trials can be as short as a few hours or as
long as a few weeks or months, depending on the complexity of the case and
the number of witnesses being called. Trials occur in both civil and criminal
cases. A *civil* lawsuit means that one private party (a person or a business, called
the *plaintiff*) has sued another (called the *defendant*), usually trying to get

money or an order forcing the other party to do something. A *criminal* lawsuit is brought by the state or federal government (the *prosecution*) against someone who has broken the law (the *defendant*).

Both sides begin with an *opening statement* that tells the jury what they expect will come out during the trial. The parties then present their *case-in-chief*, in which they tell their respective sides of the story through witnesses and exhibits. After both sides have presented their cases, the attorneys give *closing arguments*, combining the law with the facts that came out during trial to argue that their client should win. In each element of the trial, the prosecution/plaintiff presents first, since it is the side with the burden of proof.[1] Here's a quick look at the major components of a trial:

The Stages of a Trial

- Jury Selection (*Voir Dire*)

  The attorneys for both sides question prospective jurors to determine whether they are fit to serve on the jury. Most states require 12-person juries, but some permit smaller juries. A trial practice class may skip the step of jury selection because your classmates serve as jurors.

- **Opening Statements**

  Both sides explain their theory of what happened. Attorneys give a preview of what their key witnesses will say, and tell the jury what to look for when listening to witnesses and considering the evidence.

- **Prosecution/Plaintiff's Case-in-Chief**

  ○ *Direct Examination.* The prosecution/plaintiff calls witnesses that support its case. An attorney for the prosecution/plaintiff questions each witness using open-ended questions that allow the witness to do most of the talking. A direct examination should sound like a conversation that the jury gets to hear.

  ○ *Cross-Examination.* A defense attorney questions the witnesses using leading questions to elicit facts that the witness will have difficulty disputing. This allows the defense to call into question the witness's testimony on direct examination, or to point out other facts that help the defense.

---

1. The party with the *burden of persuasion or proof* is the side that has to prove the elements of a claim in order to win. For example, in a criminal case, the government bears the burden of proving the defendant guilty, but the defendant is not required to prove himself innocent. If the government cannot meet its burden, the defendant goes free.

- **Defense's Case-in-Chief**
  - *Direct Examination.* The defense calls witnesses that are favorable to its case or that rebut testimony elicited by the prosecution/plaintiff.
  - *Cross-Examination.* An attorney for the prosecution/plaintiff questions defense witnesses on weaknesses in their testimony or to elicit positive facts for the prosecution/plaintiff.
- **Closing Arguments**
  Both sides explain what legal issues are at stake and lay out the elements the prosecution/plaintiff had to prove. Attorneys recap the facts that came out during trial, and argue why those facts do or don't allow the plaintiff/prosecution to meet its burden of proof.
- **Rebuttal**
  Many jurisdictions allow the prosecution/plaintiff to reserve time for rebuttal following the defense's closing argument. This is one last opportunity for the plaintiff/prosecution to persuade the jury by confronting the strongest points the defense made during its closing argument.
- **Jury Deliberations**
  The jury discusses the case in private and decides which side wins, or determines verdicts for each criminal charge. Most states require a unanimous jury verdict in a criminal case. A jury that cannot reach a unanimous decision is called a *hung jury*, and the prosecution has the option to retry the defendant in this situation. Some jurisdictions require a unanimous verdict in a civil case, while others permit a verdict to be returned in a civil case with some dissenting votes.

If you take a trial practice class, you will learn the nuts and bolts of how to make an opening statement and a closing argument, and how to question witnesses properly. Repetition is the best way to drill these skills into your brain so that you can perform well under pressure, and many students focus much of their energy on the minutia of getting these details correct. But convincing a jury requires more than just mastering the mechanics—you have to understand the big picture of how to tell a compelling story. The lessons of rhetoric discussed in Chapter Four can help you transform yourself from a competent advocate into an extraordinary one. Here's how those lessons apply in trials.

The Importance of Credibility (*Ethos*)

As we discussed in Chapter Four, rhetoricians have long known that audiences are more likely to be persuaded by speakers they believe have good character, or *ethos*. Trials may strain your ability to appear credible because you are performing under stress, often with very little sleep. You want to win, and you may find yourself reacting defensively and in desperation if something unexpected arises during the course of the proceedings. But you must keep your cool. Exhibiting ethos under pressure is essential to persuading a jury of the soundness of your case.

What else can you do to show you are credible? The first step is to master all the facts of your case. You must know the *record* (the transcripts of what the witnesses have said and all the evidence) cold. If it's clear that you know every word of every deposition and the details about every exhibit, and that you have given thought to what you need to prove and how you're going to incorporate the supporting evidence, then you will be able to handle motions and objections with ease. The jury will trust you more because you will project confidence and competence.

Another key to establishing ethos: Don't exaggerate. If in the heat of the moment you state everything in the extreme — "That witness is the worst liar I have ever seen!" — then the jury is less likely to believe you. It's too easy to disprove an inflated claim, especially one that's offered in an overheated way. If you say that your client is a great person, for example, and the record contains ample evidence that the guy cheated on his wife, dodged his creditors, and abused his pets, then you can be sure that opposing counsel will point out the discrepancy. Your client's credibility will suffer, but yours will deteriorate as well.

To build credibility, you should also follow the "rule of restraint," which teaches that, in order to be persuasive, you need to figure out the heart of your case and focus on it. Resist the temptation to muck around with something that's not central to what you must prove, because if you do the judge or jury may end up doubting your entire case. For example, imagine that you are arguing a breach of contract case involving an agreement between two companies, in which you must prove that one company did not hold up its end of the bargain. The motives or character of the people involved are neither here nor there — if you can prove that the contract was violated, you win. So if you spend a good bit of your time trying to paint the owner of the breaching company as an evil villain, you run the risk that a juror will think, "He doesn't seem like such a bad guy" — and find against you as a result.

Be careful not to misstate facts or leave out those that hurt your case, because inevitably the law student or lawyer on the other side will bring them up. If the jury realizes you conveniently omitted evidence that disproves your point, you've eroded your ethos. (On the other hand, if the student arguing the other side of your case misstates facts, you have an opportunity. Consider creating a terrific visual aid that you could use in closing argument, putting his actual words on a chart, with the testimony disproving his claims right next to it.)

Tone is central to ethos. In the heat of the battle of a trial, many law students (and lawyers, too) adopt an aggressive, sarcastic tone, belittling witnesses and opposing counsel alike. But an overheated tone leaves you nowhere to go. If you have displayed outrage during your cross-examination of every witness, for example, then you have no emotion to reach for when you encounter evidence in a later examination that actually is outrageous.

Beware also of going too far in the other direction—while you don't want to be a bully, you also don't want to seem like a pushover. If you mumble, hesitate, fumble with exhibits, and use passive body language, the jury will believe you lack confidence in your case and yourself. (See Chapter Four for a detailed discussion of using body language to project confidence.)

Engage the Jury's Attention (*Pathos*)

Another important method of persuasion (discussed also in Chapter Four), is *pathos*, or engaging the audience's emotions. You must figure out how to get the jury connected to your client and your case. The first step towards this goal is figuring out how to explain your client's side through a believable and engaging story that jurors will want to hear. Lawyers call this story the *theory of the case.*

Your case will be much more interesting and coherent if you have a central theory, which will be the theme you will build your entire presentation around. For example, think about the breach of contract case we discussed above—two companies, a contract, one violated it, the other is suing. Summarize what happened in a single sentence in a way that presents your argument. That's your theory of the case.

If you are like many lawyers, you may have come up with a theory of the case that sounds something like, "This is a case about a breach of contract." That's an accurate statement, and it is pithy, so it's a good first step. But there are no human beings in that version, and you can't tell who did what to whom. It also contains jargon. Most people don't know what "breach of contract" means,[2] nor do they care. People don't care about breaches, or contracts, and

---

2. In fact, you might not know what it means if you are reading this book before taking a contracts class. *Breach of contract* means that there are two parties (which could be people or companies), they have an agreement (often written, but not always), and one didn't do what he was supposed to under the agreement, so the other sued.

very often they don't care about companies. People tend to care most about other people.

So we'll look for some people to put into the story. Let's imagine that one of the companies is a craft shop owned by a woman named Maureen Moss. The other is a fire insurance company that sold Ms. Moss a policy, which means the company agreed to compensate Ms. Moss for damages in the event of a fire. There's been a fire, and now the company refuses to pay.

You are representing the craft store, and you want to tell a story that includes people and makes clear who did what. So now your theory of the case is, "This is a case about Maureen Moss, who owns a small craft store in town, and about the fire insurance company that broke its promise to her and let her down when she needed it most." Now you even have a refrain that you could use — "broken promises." Much better.

People care more about things they can visualize or imagine. As you write your opening statement or closing argument, or as you question witnesses about events, take the time to paint a verbal picture of anything you want the jury to remember. Make sure they know what the craft store looked like, what it felt like to work there, and how terrifying the fire was when it broke out. Create a movie in their minds that will stick with them when they retire to the jury room to reach their verdict.

Use visual aids, like exhibits and diagrams, to make your points more vivid, and linger on them during the trial so the images really sink in. People are much more likely to remember information that they both hear and see. If you have an exhibit that helps your case, go through the necessary steps to get it admitted into evidence (explained later), but don't stop there. Make sure the jury can see the exhibit, which may mean making copies of it or bringing it closer to them. Have a witness talk about the exhibit so that the jury understands the significance of it. And then show it to them again during your closing argument.

Finally, invoking pathos demands conviction and flair from you. You have to convey to the jury that you believe in your case, and that you care about it. Re-read Chapter Four for suggestions about how to use your pace, tone, voice, and physicality to bring your presentation to life.

Persuade Them with Logic (*Logos*)

The jury has to understand the logic of your story, and how the testimony and pieces of evidence prove your case. It's not enough to examine witnesses on the stand or successfully have evidence admitted into the record — you have to make connections for jurors so they understand why the facts add up in your favor. This is an exercise of logic, or *logos*.

Put yourself in the shoes of the jury, and think about what they do and don't know. The import of a particular piece of evidence may be perfectly clear to you because you have spent time thinking about it, but you'll need to spell out this implication for the jury in a clear, strong argument because otherwise it may not be obvious to them. Slow down as you explain any complicated evidence or argument, because jurors need time to process what they are hearing. In fact, you may want to cover important points several times — perhaps through the testimony of a couple of witnesses, and then again during your closing argument.

Your closing argument offers a great opportunity to recap and reinforce the logic of your case. To use it to your best advantage, spend a lot of time crafting it, following the rules outlined in Chapter Four for writing a presentation. You should write your closing argument long before the trial starts, then tweak it as the trial progresses to take into account the actual testimony and exhibits that are elicited during trial. The closing argument should drive home your theory of the case. Choose a simple, clear structure and words that are easy for the jury to understand, and make the logic even more accessible by using visual aids where necessary.

Now that you have considered a rhetorical overview, let's turn to the nuts and bolts of trials.

The Opening Statement

Trials begin with lawyers on both sides making an *opening statement* laying out their versions of the facts of the case, and telling the jury about the witnesses that they can expect to hear once the testimony begins. The length of the opening statement depends on how complicated the case is, and in a trial practice class the instructor will tell you how long yours should be. Since opening statements mark the beginning of a trial, they typically are the first skill that you will learn in a trial practice class. You start to establish your ethos here, as this is the first impression you'll make on the jury. This is also a moment that jurors are likely to pay attention to and remember, so you should drive home your theory of the case right away.

Opening statements are challenging writing exercises, though, because of an odd rule of court — you are not allowed to argue during an opening statement. You are simply supposed to offer the jury a preview of the facts you expect to bring out during the course of the trial, and of the witnesses who will testify. You aren't permitted to tell the jury what you think the facts mean, or to suggest any conclusion or inference from them.

This is a strange, constraining rule because we draw conclusions from things in normal conversation all the time. It's perfectly natural in everyday life to say things like, "That's not fair," or "It doesn't make sense," or "I don't believe it." But during a trial you have to save all those rhetorical flourishes for the closing argument.

Here's an example of a permissible opening statement on behalf of Maureen Moss and her craft shop. The witnesses who will testify to the facts you are laying out are indicated in brackets.

> Ladies and gentlemen of the jury, this is a case about Maureen Moss, who owns Crafty Crafts, a small craft store here in town, and about the fire insurance company that broke its promise to her and let her down when she needed them the most. [**Theory of the case** — it's usually okay **to present this at the beginning of an opening, even though some conservative judges might rule it argument.**]
>
> You are going to meet Ms. Moss and some of her employees, and you are going to hear those employees talk about how much care and pride Ms. Moss took in Crafty Crafts. You are going to hear about the care that she took in running her business, in hiring her employees, and in caring for and maintaining her shop. [**Testimony of employees Anna Anderson and John Franklin.**] And you are going to hear about how, when Walter Smith from the Assure Fire Insurance Company came to see Ms. Moss two years ago and told her that her current fire insurance wasn't adequate for her business, she took that advice very seriously. Ms. Moss herself will tell you that she felt horrified that she might have underinsured her shop, and grateful that Mr. Smith explained that to her. And she bought a policy from him. [**Testimony of Maureen Moss.**]
>
> Fast forward two years, and you will hear about a terrible fire that engulfed Crafty Crafts. The shop was full of highly flammable craft materials, plus the building was made of wood and was nearly 70 years old. You will hear that it went up in flames—whoosh!—just like that. And you will hear from a fire expert that there is nothing left. Not a thing. He will tell you it is impossible to know with certainty what started the fire because everything is gone. [**Testimony of expert James Jones.**]
>
> You will also hear about what happened after the fire. You will learn that Ms. Moss called Walter Smith to file her claim the day the fire happened. You will learn that he did not answer his phone, so she left him a message. And another one the next day. And another one the day after that. She called seven times in all, and each time she either got his voicemail or was told he was unavailable. She also e-mailed him three times, but he never replied to those e-mails. The first time that Ms. Moss heard

back from Assure Fire was when she received a letter from them six months after the fire, denying her claim. [**Testimony of Maureen Moss.**] You will also learn that at the time Mr. Smith sent Ms. Moss that letter, no one from Assure Fire had visited the site of the fire, or interviewed Ms. Moss or any of the employees from Crafty Crafts. [**Testimony of Gerald Brown, fire investigator for Assure Fire.**]

Ms. Moss needs Assure Fire to keep its promise to her, and to pay her the proceeds of the policy, so that she can start to rebuild. Ladies and gentlemen, at the end of this trial, we will come back to you and ask you to hold Assure Fire to its promise. We will ask you to find that they must pay Ms. Moss the money that she is due. Thank you.

Notice that every fact in the opening can be linked to a particular witness, and there are no interpretations of facts. Here is a similar opening, but with impermissible argument in it:

Ladies and gentlemen of the jury, this is a case about Maureen Moss, who owns Crafty Crafts, a small craft store here in town, and about the fire insurance company that broke its promise to her and let her down when she needed them the most.

Maureen Moss would never burn down her own store. She's not that kind of person. You will hear from several of her employees who will tell you that she loved her store more than anything, and that there is no way she would destroy it. [**Objectionable — drawing conclusions.**]

In fact, the wrongdoer here is clearly Assure Fire Insurance Company. You will meet Walter Smith, the man from Assure Fire who sold Ms. Moss the policy in the first place. [**That sentence is okay.**] He tried to sell her as big a policy as possible in order to take as much of her money as he could [**objectionable**], and now that there's been a fire, he and his company won't pay [**that phrase is okay**]. In fact, they're doing everything they can to get out of paying [**objectionable**]. When she called him to tell him about the fire, Walter Smith dodged her calls, didn't call her back, wouldn't reply to e-mails, and finally sent a letter denying the claim without even examining the premises. [**That sentence is okay.**] You can tell from these actions that he and his company are acting in bad faith. [**Objectionable.**]

These may be obvious conclusions to include in your closing argument, but they are not allowed in an opening statement. You can (and should) line up your facts so that your conclusions become clear, but you cannot actually draw those conclusions at this point in the proceedings.

A word about body language in opening statements: You will be more credible if you step away from the lectern and deliver your opening statement standing directly in front of jurors, looking them in the eye. Don't read the opening statement from your notes. Follow the tips about body language discussed in Chapter Four. An opening statement is a classic formal presentation, and requires confident body language.

Direct Examination

After opening statements, the plaintiff (in a civil trial) or the prosecution (in a criminal trial) begins to prove its case by calling witnesses to tell its side of the story. The witness answers the attorney's questions, a process called *direct examination*.

During direct examination, you are essentially the voice of the jury, so ask questions jurors would want to know answers to, and do it in an order that makes sense. If a witness says something interesting—"I was scared!"—then follow up with "Why were you scared?" rather than the next question on your list ("Where did you go to school?").

Give some thought to which witnesses you want to call to the stand and why. You don't have to call every single person who has a connection to the case. In a real trial, you'll spend a significant amount of time before the trial begins taking *depositions* of witnesses (questioning them under oath, with the exchange transcribed by a court reporter). Depositions are a time to learn what a witness knows and what really happened, and they also show you how the witness will appear to the jury. In our hypothetical craft store case, if you have two witnesses who can establish the fact that Maureen Moss loved her shop and would never burn it down, but one of those witnesses is disreputable in some way (has a criminal record or comes off like a jerk), then don't call the problematic witness. Call the solid witness instead.

As you prepare to build your case, it can be a helpful to write down your theory of the case, your proof to support that theory, and how each witness will shore up or reinforce that theory. Have a list of the testimony you absolutely must elicit from each witness, and bring that list with you up to the lectern during questioning so you don't forget anything. Plan the order of your witnesses in a way that helps present a credible story to the jury. You're not allowed to tell the jury why you called a witness, but the reasons will come out when you ask him the right questions.

Typically, your direct examination would begin with a few questions that establish who the witness is, her connection to the case, and why she is credible (for example, establishing that Anna Anderson is an employee at Crafty Crafts, that she knows Maureen Moss well, and that she was the person who locked up on the night of the fire, so she can describe the condition of the premises that night). Then you ask questions that allow the witness to tell her story. Try to give this story some structure to make it more memorable. For example, you could organize Anna Anderson's testimony by time period—the period before the fire (establishing what a responsible person Maureen is and how much care she took with her business), the events on the day of the fire (establishing that nothing suspicious transpired), and the period after the fire (establishing that no one's been able to find work, and so all the Crafty Crafts employees are much worse off because of the fire).

In direct examination you are not permitted to ask *leading questions*. A leading question is one that suggests its own answer, such as, "You went to work, didn't you?" (An acceptable alternative would be, "Where did you go?") Getting the form of the question right may take practice because in everyday life we ask leading questions all the time. Until you become an expert in direct examination, write your questions in advance to make sure they aren't leading. If you start each question with "who," "what," "where," "when," "how" or "explain," your question is probably okay.

During direct examination, your witness is the star. You are playing a supporting role—gently feeding him the short, non-leading questions that will help him tell his story, one fact at a time. You should stand behind the lectern as you question the witness, because you want the jury's eyes to be on your witness, not on you. Encourage your witness to look the jurors in the eye by reminding him that he is speaking to them. ("Please tell the jury what you saw next.") Jurors are more likely to believe facts if they hear it from the witness's mouth, not yours, so keep your questions short and clear so that the witness does most of the talking.

You should, however, ensure that the story makes sense. Sometimes witnesses attach significance to things that are simply beside the point. For example, perhaps Anna Anderson hated the uniform she had to wear and would love to testify about that—since it has nothing to do with the case, you can circumvent the whole topic through careful questioning.

Sometimes witnesses are nervous and blurt out their stories so quickly that the jury can't absorb them. You can help slow down the pace by asking the witness about events in increments or by circling back to ask follow-up questions. For example, imagine you ask Anna Anderson about the night of the fire and she says, "I locked up and went home. That's it." But you need to show that Maureen required the employees to follow a methodical system for closing up for the day, including making sure the coffee pot was turned off to prevent a fire. To slow Anna down to elicit more details, you can ask her single-fact questions (her likely answers are noted in brackets):

- What time did the store close the day of the fire? [6 p.m.]
- Who was there at closing time? [Just me.]
- Tell us about what you do to lock up for the day. How do you know what to do? [Maureen makes us use this checklist.] (*Get checklist entered into evidence.*)
- What's first on your checklist? [Well, first I lock the door so no one else comes in.]
- Then what do you do? [Then I put out the "closed" sign.]
- What comes next? [Then I have to do kitchen inspection.]
- What does kitchen inspection mean? [Well, I turn off the coffee pot, wash any dishes we used, take out the trash, that sort of thing.]
- Why do you turn off the coffee pot? [So there's no fire.]
- Did you turn off the coffee pot the night of the fire? [I don't remember—I was in a hurry.]

By the way, it's a bad idea to give the witness a script of what you want her to say. That script may be discoverable[3] under the Federal Rules of Evidence[4] because it is material that the witness used to prepare to testify. Plus you will end up with a witness who sounds phony. But it's perfectly fine—encouraged, even—to meet your witness in advance of direct examination to let her practice answering your questions and learn more about what you want to ask. Reassure her that you'll ask her the right questions, so she doesn't have to memorize anything. In fact, if she can't remember, you can help her by refreshing her recollection (see "Direct Examination Techniques: Refreshing a Witness's Recollection"). All she has to do is to tell the truth. You also can help your witness enormously by asking clear and direct questions, and indicating your confidence in her through your tone during the interrogation.

---

3. *Discoverable* means that the material must be given to opposing counsel. If you find yourself having to turn your direct examination script over to opposing counsel, he will have a huge strategic advantage.

4. Trial practice classes typically use the Federal Rules of Evidence, which is what you would use in federal court. If you appear in state court, you would follow the rules of evidence of that state.

Direct Examination Techniques:
Refreshing a Witness's Recollection

Sometimes a witness will become so terrified on the stand that she cannot remember something she used to know. If that happens to your witness, the rules of court permit you to refresh her recollection. You can use anything that might jog the witness's memory—a transcript of a deposition that she gave about the events in question, or notes she might have made, for example. If your witness draws a blank, here's what to do:

- (Establish that she's forgotten.) Ms. Moss, can you remember what the date of the meeting was? [No.]
- Is there something that I could show you that would refresh your recollection? [Yes, my desk calendar.]
- (Hand the witness the desk calendar, let her look at the date, then take the calendar away.) Now, testifying with a refreshed recollection, can you tell us when the meeting occurred?

Direct Examination Techniques:
Entering an Exhibit into Evidence

Documents or other pieces of physical evidence very often can help prove your case. The judge must admit them into evidence before the jury can look at them, and they are labeled as exhibits in order to make it clear in the record (the written transcript of the case) which item you are talking about. Exhibits can help drive home a witness's testimony because they make a point more vividly than testimony alone can.

To enter a document into evidence—for example, the fire department's report about the fire at Crafty Crafts—you must establish that the document is what you are claiming it is, a process called authentication. This process typically is done during direct examination. Generally, the witness authenticating the exhibit should be someone with knowledge of it, such as the firefighter who wrote the report. Once the party entering the exhibit has laid the appropriate foundation, the other party has an opportunity to make an evidentiary objection (an objection based on the rules of evidence). Here is a basic script authenticating and entering a piece of documentary evidence:

- (Approach opposing counsel and give him a copy of the document.) Let the record reflect I am showing opposing counsel Plaintiff's Exhibit 1.
- May I approach the witness? (Give him a copy of the document.)
- Let the record reflect I am handing the witness a document that has been marked Plaintiff's Exhibit 1 for identification.
- Fire Chief Ross, do you recognize this document? [I do.]
- Can you tell us what it is? [It is the fire report about the fire that occurred at Crafty Crafts on January 12, 2012.]
- Who is the author of this report? [I am.]

- When did you write this report? [Some of it I wrote the night of the fire, January 12, and the rest I wrote the next day.]
- Is this a record kept in the regular course of your duties as fire chief?[5] [Yes.]
- Does this appear to be a fair and accurate copy of the report? [Yes.]
- Your honor, at this time we tender Plaintiff's Exhibit 1 into evidence. (Once it has been admitted, give a copy to each member of the jury so they can see it, and then question the witness about the document so the jury can see why it's important.)

Sometimes you will need to enter a tangible object, such as a piece of physical evidence found at the scene of the incident. Suppose you are the attorney for Assure Fire Insurance, and you would like to enter into evidence a can of paint thinner (a fire accelerant) that the fire inspector found near Crafty Crafts the day after the store burned down. Simply laying foundation that the fire inspector found a can of paint thinner will not be enough. Instead, you will need to establish that this is the same can that the fire inspector found:

- Can you describe the can of paint thinner you found near the scene? [It was a rectangular metal can — a brand called "PaintAway."]
- Would you recognize the can of paint thinner if I showed it to you? [Yes, I would.]
- (Approach opposing counsel) Let the record reflect I am showing opposing counsel what has been previously marked for identification as Defense Exhibit A.
- May I approach the witness?
- (Hand him exhibit.) Let the record reflect I am handing the witness Defense Exhibit A. What is this? [It's the can of paint thinner that I found.]
- How can you tell it's the same can? [It has "Crafty Crafts" written on the bottom of it in permanent marker — just like the one I found. It's also the same brand — PaintAway. When I found it, I marked it with that evidence sticker that you see affixed to the bottom and wrote my initials and the date on that sticker. I then locked it in our evidence room. I retrieved the can from the evidence room to bring it to the courtroom today.]
- At this time we tender Defense Exhibit A into evidence.

---

5. These questions are included because a fire department report is technically *hearsay*, or an out-of-court statement being entered for its truth. In general, hearsay is prohibited because we prefer that witnesses testify firsthand about what they saw. Prohibiting hearsay allows jurors to evaluate the credibility of the speaker, and prevents the use of unreliable statements that weren't made under oath. But there are numerous exceptions to the hearsay rule, and if you can show that an out-of-court statement falls within one of those exceptions, you can get it admitted into evidence. The hearsay rule includes an exception for public records like a fire department report in the Federal Rules of Evidence. *See* FRE 803(8) (reprinted in the Appendix at the end of this book). In order to qualify for the exception, the document must be a record or statement of a public office setting out a matter observed while under a legal duty to report, provided that neither the source of the information nor other circumstances indicate a lack of trustworthiness.

Cross-Examination

After one side has conducted the direct examination of a witness, opposing counsel is allowed to conduct a cross-examination of the witness. This is another question-and-answer exchange, but with the goal of highlighting weaknesses in the witness's testimony.

In order to perform cross-examination effectively, you have to master every fact in the case, and in particular, every bit of the witness's prior writings and testimony. *You should only ask questions to which you already know the answer.* Typically, a witness in a case has given a deposition before the trial or perhaps was interrogated by the police. Use these materials to find statements that show the witness is biased or could not have seen what she claims to have seen, and also keep an eye out for any place that the witness has changed her story. For example, imagine that you are cross-examining Anna Anderson, who has testified that Maureen Moss would never in a million years burn down her craft store. You know from Anna's deposition that she only worked for Maureen for six months, that she does not know Maureen outside of the workplace, and that she does not know the details of Maureen's personal life. Your cross-examination could proceed as follows to make those points:

- Ms. Anderson, you only worked for Maureen Moss for the six months leading up to the fire, is that correct?
- And prior to that time, you didn't know Maureen Moss?
- Your relationship with her was a professional one?
- You didn't socialize with her after work?
- And in fact, you don't know much about Maureen Moss's personal life, do you?
- For example, you weren't aware that Ms. Moss has a gambling problem, were you?
- And you didn't know that Ms. Moss had borrowed over $100,000 to cover her gambling losses, did you?

Now, in an everyday conversation, you might be tempted to ask a question to which you do not know the answer, such as, "Does the fact that she's in so much debt change your mind about whether she started the fire?" Resist that temptation. The questions you've already asked show that Anna doesn't have all the facts, so her opinion of whether Maureen burned down the store has little value. And you've also used the cross-examination to highlight your theory of the case—that Maureen Moss is a desperate woman leading a shady double life, and she burned down the store as a last-ditch effort to get out of a financial bind. If you ask that ultimate question, you're giving Anna room to say, "Oh,

I know she would NEVER do such a thing!" and then to spin some compelling story that the jury will never forget. Don't try to draw conclusions with the witness still on the stand. Save it for closing argument.

During cross-examination, you have a powerful tool at your disposal — the leading question. Use it. A leading question is one that suggests its own answer. The preceding cross-examination was structured so that Anna would simply answer "yes" to each question. The focus during cross-examination should stay on you, the lawyer. You are telling the story through your questions, which are essentially short, single fact sentences with "true?" or "isn't that right?" or simply a question mark tacked on to the end. If you design the questions well (for example, tracking exactly what the witness already said during a deposition), then the witness will have little choice but to agree with you.

As with all parts of the trial, the tone that you use during cross-examination is extremely important. Cross-examination can be stressful because the witness may be hostile or give you an unexpected answer, or because you may be nervous. Sometimes this causes lawyers and law students to adopt an overly aggressive tone in an effort to control the witness, or to stand too close to a witness in an effort to intimidate him. This can backfire if the jury perceives you as a bully. Instead, stay behind the lectern (where you need to be anyway so that you can look at your notes), and try a tone of calm confidence. Even when you are proving that a witness is lying, a tone that shows calm professionalism and expertise will appeal to a jury more than one that suggests you enjoy humiliating someone. You may occasionally need to be tough with a witness, but beware of reaching for an aggressive tone if it is uncalled for. If you do, you will have no room to bring on the tough stuff when you actually need it.

Impeaching a Witness

On cross-examination, attorneys attempt to "impeach," or call into question, the credibility of the other side's witnesses. You might do this by showing that an important eyewitness was hiding behind a wall when the events occurred and didn't actually see anything. If the witness has a history of lying, you could ask questions that make the jury wonder whether the witness is telling the truth in this case. It's also a good idea to point out any bias the witness might have, such as if he's a friend of the party calling him to testify or is an expert being paid for his time in court.

The most complex form of impeachment—but often the most damaging for the witness's credibility—uses a prior inconsistent statement by that witness, typically found in a deposition or an *affidavit* (a statement written by the witness under oath in which the witness is told to include all relevant information).

Since the witness was under oath when making these prior statements, it's a major blow to his credibility if he contradicts that statement during his trial testimony. Successfully impeaching a witness with a prior inconsistent statement means you have shown that the witness is lying now, has previously lied under oath, or has forgotten a critical part of his testimony. In any case, a jury is much less likely to believe what that witness has to say.

You should keep in mind, however, that most juries are reluctant to believe someone is lying to them. They are more likely to give the person the benefit of the doubt and think the witness has forgotten or is mistaken. If you are overly enthusiastic about pointing out minor contradictions or errors in the witness's testimony, jurors might resent you for being a know-it-all or beating up on an otherwise believable witness.

So make sparing use of impeachments with prior inconsistent statements. Impeach only on points that are important to your case or severely damaging to the witness's credibility. Where the witness might have testified incorrectly because he forgot, rather than because he was being misleading, gently ask if it would help if you "refresh his memory." Politely refreshing the witness's recollection will allow you to make sure the jury hears the correct facts and will still do some damage to the witness's credibility. But you will appear helpful, rather than unlikable because you played "gotcha" games with the witness.

If you believe a witness is being misleading or untruthful, and you're certain there's a line in the affidavit or deposition that directly contradicts what the witness said at trial, you can consider going forward with a full impeachment by prior inconsistent statement. Before reading the prior statement for the jury, make sure you have nailed the witness down to his contradictory statement. Repeat his contradictory answer in your next question by asking, "So it's your testimony today that _____?" If the witness knows he is playing fast and loose with his prior testimony, he often will back down and contradict himself immediately, so an impeachment with the statement will be unnecessary. If the witness maintains his position, you should proceed with the impeachment. When conducting the impeachment, make sure you are able to quickly find the line number in the deposition where the witness contradicts his testimony at trial (if you have co-counsel, he or she should help you); that you read the relevant portion of the statement to the witness rather than having the witness read it to you (if given the opportunity, some witnesses will hijack the examination and muddle your impeachment); and that you know the impeachment procedure cold so that you can skillfully make clear that the witness has contradicted himself.

Cross-Examination Techniques: Impeaching a Witness

The following script is a standard procedure for impeaching a witness using a prior inconsistent statement.

- Mr. Smith, do you remember giving a deposition in this case on [a given date]?
- That was just a few months after the events in question, wasn't it?
- And your attorney and I and a court reporter were all there, correct?
- You raised your right hand and you swore that you would tell the truth during that deposition, didn't you?
- And after you testified, you had the chance to review that testimony and correct it, didn't you?
- And then you signed it at the bottom, didn't you?
- I'm going to read a section of your deposition to you, from page X, line Y. (Make sure the witness and opposing counsel have a copy so they can read along.)
- Did I read that right?

Arguing Objections

Legal dramas like *Law & Order* often feature dramatic courtroom scenes involving a flurry of objections, where lawyers use words like "speculation" and "hearsay." You may have wondered what this jargon means, and whether real lawyers use these terms in court. Although objections in real courtrooms are often more complex than those depicted on TV, they play just as important a role in real life as they do in fictional trials.

Objections are based on the rules of evidence that govern your case. The rules of evidence are used in jury trials to ensure that all evidence the jury is allowed to hear is fair to both parties, is a reliable source of information, and is relevant to the law being argued. These rules have been developed and refined over hundreds of years of common law through judicial decisions, and have also sometimes been modified through legislative changes to state or federal law. The federal court system, like most trial practice classes, uses the Federal Rules of Evidence, or FRE. Most states also have their own sets of rules that are virtually identical to the federal rules — so once you've learned the federal rules you will also have a working knowledge of the rules in most states as well.

Many law students take a course in evidence, which teaches the Federal Rules of Evidence extensively. Although this portion of the chapter is no substitute for a full evidence course, you don't need to be an evidence scholar to learn to argue common objections that appear in mock trials and in practice. The relevant sections of the Federal Rules of Evidence discussed here appear in the Appendix at the end of the book.

Objections during trial almost always occur while a witness is being questioned or when the opposing party is trying to enter a piece of evidence into the record. If you believe the testimony or evidence violates a particular rule of evidence and is damaging to your case, you should object to try to keep the jury from hearing the evidence. To make an objection, simply stand up and say, "Objection, Your Honor," then state the grounds for the objection, such as "hearsay." If the ruling is obvious, the judge will sometimes answer immediately with "Overruled," meaning you lost the objection and the jury will be allowed to hear the evidence, or "Sustained," meaning you won the objection and the jury won't be allowed to hear the evidence. Sometimes the judge wants to hear arguments on the objection before making a ruling.

If opposing counsel is objecting to evidence you are entering, wait for opposing counsel to finish speaking. If you have an argument you want to be sure the judge considers, you can ask to weigh in by saying, "Your Honor, may I be heard?" or "Your Honor, may I respond?" Sometimes the judge will ask for a response before you have asked to make one, so you should always be prepared to argue why the evidence doesn't violate the rule cited by opposing counsel. If you are the party making the objection, listen closely to opposing counsel's response, and be prepared with a counterargument. Keep your objections and responses brief, and use plain language that is easy to follow.

As you argue objections, start with the plain language of the rule. This means having the Federal Rules of Evidence with you at all times during the trial, with the most important pages marked so that you can turn to them quickly if you need to. Think about whether opposing counsel is applying the language of the rule correctly, any exceptions to the rule, and the purpose behind the rule.

Just like other forms of public speaking, arguing objections takes practice and preparation. Before the trial starts, think about possible objections you might get to witness testimony or evidence that you're trying to enter, and how you might respond to those objections. You should also prepare for your own potential objections to evidence the opposing party may enter, and prepare counterarguments to their best responses. The table shown in Figure 2 is a helpful place to start. Here are a few of the most common objections, the rule numbers in the FRE that correspond to those objections, brief explanations of each rule, and several responses you might give to each objection.

Figure 2. Common Objections

Objection	Explanation	Common Responses
FRE 401 **Test for Relevant Evidence**	Testimony is irrelevant if it makes no fact at issue more or less probable. In other words, if it doesn't prove or disprove anything that's important to the case, it's not admissible.	• "It is the prosecution's/plaintiff's burden today to prove _____. This testimony/ evidence goes to prove/disprove that ____." • If it's about the reliability of the witness's testimony. "This goes to the credibility (or bias) of the witness."
FRE 403 **Excluding Relevant Evidence for Prejudice**	Relevant testimony is inadmissible if the risk of unfair prejudice substantially outweighs the probative value of the evidence. Relevant evidence can also be inadmissible for other reasons under Rule 403, such as that it is a waste of time or a needless presentation of cumulative evidence (meaning the jury has already heard the evidence once and need not hear it again).	• "This is extremely probative because…" • "Opposing counsel's objection goes to weight, rather than admissibility." (This means that the evidence may not mean much, but that's for the jury to decide and they should still be able to hear it.) • Needless presentation of cumulative evidence—explain why the witness needs to testify about the document (for example, it's a financial record and the witness is an accountant), then say, "We are simply highlighting for the jury the important portions of this document in order to help them understand the witness's testimony better."
FRE 404 **Character Evidence**	Evidence of a person's character or character trait is not admissible for the purpose of proving that an action conforms to character. Specific instances of conduct are admissible, however, to prove another purpose, such as intent, plan, motive, opportunity, identity, or absence of mistake or accident—or to prove an essential element of the charge, claim, or defense.	• "Specific instances of conduct are admissible to prove _____ (intent, plan, motive, etc.). This evidence does that by showing _____." • "Character evidence is admissible when a character trait is a central element of the charge/ claim/ defense…." (Then state what character trait you are offering and why it's an essential element of the charge/claim/ defense.)

Objection	Explanation	Common Responses
FRE 602 **Need for Personal Knowledge**	A witness may not testify to a matter unless sufficient foundation has been laid that the witness has personal knowledge of the matter.	• "By testifying that _____, we have already laid the foundation that the witness has personal knowledge of this fact." • "I will lay more foundation, your honor." (Then ask more questions to show that the witness has personal knowledge of the matter.)
FRE 701 **Opinion Testimony by Lay Witness**	Lay witnesses are only permitted to give their opinions when those opinions are rationally based on their perception and helpful to a clearer understanding of their testimony. They cannot speculate as to someone's mindset or thoughts.	• "This is rationally based on the perception of the witness." (Then explain how what the witness observed matches what the witness deduced from the situation). • If your witness is an expert: "This witness is an expert in the field of _____, and can therefore testify as to his/her professional opinion on these matters."
FRE 702 **Testimony by Expert Witnesses**	Before a witness can offer an expert opinion, the party offering the opinion must establish that the witness is qualified to give expert testimony in that field. The witness must also have sufficient facts and data to form the opinion, have used reliable principles and methods, and have applied those methods reliably to this case.	• "We have established that the witness has (qualifications), and therefore has the necessary (education, training, knowledge, skill, and/or experience) to be qualified as an expert." • "We have established that the witness used methods that (have been subject to peer review, have a known error rate, are accepted within the field, etc.) and applied those methods reliably to this case, and this conclusion therefore meets the requirements of 702."
FRE 801 **Hearsay**	Any statement made outside of court that is being offered for the truth of the matter asserted.	• "We are not attempting to prove as a matter of truth that _____. Rather, this testimony goes to show…" (generally something like "the effect on the listener").

Objection	Explanation	Common Responses
FRE 801 **Hearsay** *continued*		• "This is an admission by a party opponent." • "This is an exception to hearsay under Rule 803 (or 804)…" (Then explain the exception.) • "Otherwise Inadmissible hearsay is admissible under Rule 703 as underlying facts and data of expert testimony if the probative value of the evidence substantially outweighs its danger of unfair prejudice. It's extremely important for the jury to hear this testimony so it may understand how the expert reached his conclusion that _____."

Closing Argument

After both sides have had the opportunity to make their cases, we reach closing argument. This is your chance to connect all the dots for the jury—to explain how everything they've seen and heard adds up in your favor. You are no longer constrained by the rules of opening statement; you may, and should, argue the heck out of your case. Closing argument often proves to be the most enjoyable part of a trial.

To prepare for closing argument, re-read Chapter Four and follow the rules for making a formal presentation. You should start strong, with your theory of the case; build your theme by showing how each witness and each piece of evidence adds to it; and end by empowering your jury to help your client with a just decision. Remind the jury who said what and take them through the important pieces of evidence. Make explicit the conclusions that you hinted at during your opening statement and answer the "ultimate" questions you refrained from asking on cross-examination.

Consider using an effective visual aid to show how all the pieces of evidence fit together. For example, if you are defending Assure Fire Insurance Company in Ms. Moss's suit against it, you could create a poster or chart showing the damning timing of events (see Figure 3 below).

Figure 3. Timing of Events
Moss's Gambling Debt and Insurance Policy Purchase

August 2006	Moss insured store for $200,000, kept same level of coverage for next 4 years
January-September 2010	Moss had gambling losses of $100,000
October 2010	Borrowed $100,000 to cover gambling losses at 10% interest rate; loan due in 4 months
November 2010	Tried to borrow against store, bank said no
December 2010	Increased fire insurance to $800,000
January 2011	Crafty Crafts burned down; Moss tried to cash in insurance policy

Remember that a closing argument is not only a speech, but an argument as well. The defense follows the plaintiff's or prosecution's closing argument, and the plaintiff will almost always reserve time for a brief rebuttal. Whether you are closing for the plaintiff or prosecution, or for the defense, use closing argument to respond to the other side's strongest points. Don't avoid the parts of the trial that may damage your side—confront them head-on. You might claim that even if everything the other side says is true, your client should still win, and give reasons why. You could say that the other side's case boils down to one or two key points, and refute them. Rather than jeopardizing your credibility with the jury by misrepresenting what the other side is arguing, think of the doubts you would have if you were in their shoes, and respond to those.

Closing argument is also the time to heed the lessons of ethos, pathos, and logos. You must be credible, which you will achieve through a confident delivery and coherent story. You must engage the jurors' emotions, which you will accomplish both by demonstrating power in your presentation and by getting your audience invested in your client and your cause. And you must persuade the jury through logic, which requires clear language, visual aids (usually), and a carefully structured explanation of your theory of the case.

Chapter Seven

Leading a Student Organization

Participating in student organizations can make law school a richer experience. Student organizations can be tremendous fun and offer you the chance to meet new people who may become important business contacts in the future. There is nothing quite like bonding with classmates as you work together to get a law journal published on time or organize a conference — you may be surprised to find that these relationships are the ones that you call on time and again during the course of your career. Getting involved in a student organization is also an excellent way to expand your skill set so that you are more desirable to potential employers.

The Benefits of Leadership Experience

Many of the students I interviewed reported that the experience of leading a student organization is invaluable. You'll learn how to manage and work with other people and lead projects and meetings — skills that lawyers must cultivate. If you develop your management ability while you are still in school, you can work out the kinks in your leadership style without your boss looking on. To become an effective leader, verbal skills are once again key.

Karin is a young attorney who founded a student organization while she was still in college. Her organization, which focused on fostering the leadership skills of conservative women, was controversial on her college campus. She continued leading the organization throughout law school, and expanded it to numerous campuses across the country.

Karin found that the hours she logged as the leader of her organization paid her dividends when she entered the job market. She was confident and articulate during interviews because she often had to speak in public to promote the work of her club, and she was impassioned about the organization's mission. Even employers who did not share her conservative roots respected her drive, her intelligence, and her enthusiasm. Her job search consequently was quite successful.

One of Karin's strengths is her ability to deal effectively with conflict, a skill she attributes to her experience as a student leader. She tells the story of when students with political views opposing hers came to harass the women's book club she organized:

> During my fourth year of college, I was running this conservative women's book club and some liberal guys came to one of our meetings. When they showed up, I had to decide how to respond. I could've asked them to leave the meeting, but I just didn't think that was the way to handle it at the time. We started our meeting, we welcomed them, and we shared our cookies with them. We were discussing a chapter of a book, like we did at all our meetings — and pretty soon they were purposely asking controversial questions and trying to stir things up. I let things play out, and one of our members who is small — maybe 5-foot — every time they started asking questions, she'd just respond calmly with answers based on things that we had read. Their questions started a conversation, and it was really interesting. I would say when you're leading an organization, there are going to be some unexpected things that come up, and it's important to evaluate your options, and not jump the gun too soon. Think about what you want to do and trust your ability to handle it. Looking back, this turned out to be one of those unexpectedly cool moments.

Rather than panicking, Karin found that she was able to lead a valuable meeting while allowing her guests to express alternative viewpoints. The discourse remained civil because she herself set the tone by welcoming the newcomers and offering them food. She resisted the temptation to shut things down or to jump in too quickly in an attempt to control things; instead, she trusted her ability and those of her fellow club members to discuss their ideas in a potentially hostile environment. Because the club members remained calm and spoke respectfully, the visitors responded in kind and both sides were able to engage in a productive conversation. They might not have left that meeting in agreement about the book, but they were able to have an exchange that Karin still remembers as meaningful. That's a valuable lesson that many lawyers struggle to learn, but Karin started her legal career knowing that she didn't have to shrink from conflict.

How to Lead a Meeting

During your time in a student organization, you will probably experience a poorly led meeting. It might be a meeting where nothing is accomplished, where things run on for hours over schedule, or where tempers flare and members quit. If you're the person leading a meeting, there are things you can do to ensure that it runs smoothly.

Prepare an Agenda in Advance

Before the meeting happens, think about the purpose of the meeting and what you hope to accomplish. Each meeting should have at least one goal. Running a successful meeting is similar to writing a successful speech — you need a theme (the thing you hope to accomplish at the meeting), and you need a clear structure that the participants can follow. Every person at the meeting will feel more secure about your leadership if they can see that you have considered in advance why you are meeting and how you will accomplish your goals.

Once you have figured out your plan and goals, type this up as the agenda for the meeting and circulate it in advance to anyone attending, especially anyone expected to speak at the meeting. Estimate time limits for each item.

A sample agenda might look like this:

Law Review Meeting

Note: If you want to be sure we talk about your issue, e-mail the Editor-in-Chief in advance to be added to the agenda.

1. Call to order, introduction of new member (5 minutes)
2. Managing editors report on work assignments for next two weeks (15 minutes)
3. Notes editor reports on mentoring meetings for student note submissions (10 minutes)
4. Articles editor reports on recently accepted articles (10 minutes)
5. Social Committee reports on sign-ups for holiday party duties (10 minutes)
6. Floor open to members to raise other business (10 minutes)

Respect People's Time

Start and end the meeting on time. If some members of the group aren't present at the start of the meeting, begin without them. Consider ordering the agenda so that the topic people care about most is the first thing you discuss, and tell them you will begin on time so they will be motivated to be punctual. You may have members who are late to the first couple of meetings you run, but if you always begin on time, you'll find that people are more likely to arrive on time. If you always wait for everyone to straggle in, then people will learn that the real start time of the meeting is 15 minutes after the published start time.

Similarly, students at the meeting will take their allotted time limits more seriously if you enforce them. Warn those who will be speaking during the meeting that they will be cut off if they exceed their allotted time. That may sound harsh, and you may meet some resistance at first, but over time your members will learn to take time limits seriously, and most attendees will appreciate the fact that you are not wasting time. It might take a few attempts for you to accurately gauge how long it will take to get through a particular topic, but you'll find that you become better at managing time the more you pay attention to it. You might bring a stopwatch with you to the meeting, or make sure that you are wearing a watch or have a clock in the room. After several meetings, you'll get a feel for how long a particular block of time has run, which will help you realize when to move things along. Cutting people off can feel awkward — the trick is to do it with some charm and gentle humor. ("Okay, Bill, we've got three minutes left — how about giving us the take-home points?") You can cut someone a little slack if it turns out you legitimately underestimated the time it would take to get through a topic. But then pay particular attention to estimating the time better at the next meeting.

You can also tell it's time to move to the next agenda item when you find yourself feeling weary, or when you notice other members of the organization appearing restless. Just like you would for a speech, pay attention to the body language of your audience and keep things rolling to make the meeting successful.

Respecting people's time also means ending the meeting on time. If a topic isn't on the agenda, it shouldn't be included in the meeting. If you don't enforce this rule, your meeting may be shanghaied unexpectedly by someone who wants to talk about something off-topic.

Consider What Should Be Accomplished Outside of a Meeting

Some items are better dealt with outside of the meeting, because if all organization members chime in about every single thing, nothing will ever get done. You might assign particular tasks to groups of officers or committees, and ask the group to prepare a short report (give them a time limit) that they will present at the meeting. Or ask the organization's members to e-mail you their thoughts about a topic in advance, and tell them that you will compile the responses and start the meeting with a summary of the various viewpoints of the group. This can help things progress much more quickly than if you allow every attendee to opine about every item during the meeting itself.

Keep the Meeting Productive and the Conversation on Track

A meeting will feel successful to attendees if you are able to accomplish what you set out to do, if you have managed the time well, and if each person feels like they have had an opportunity to be heard.

Think about what kinds of questions will encourage a useful discussion. For example, if you convene a meeting and ask something open-ended and vague, directed at no one in particular ("So, a holiday party—what do you guys think?"), you may be met with silence and blank stares, and will waste time. Instead, turn your question into something specific ("So, you've all been asked to e-mail Ben your ideas for the holiday party. Ben, can you please tell us about which idea won and what we need to do now to make it happen?"). This skill is similar to one that you will develop when you take depositions in a case, or question a witness in court. If you ask a precise, thought-out question, you will elicit a more meaningful answer.

Sometimes groups can benefit from brainstorming sessions. Even this seemingly uncontrolled exercise requires your leadership. Announce the ground rules up front: "Let's brainstorm now about how we're going to raise some money. We'll take the next 15 minutes just to shout out ideas. Don't worry if you haven't thought them out; just share them. I'll write every idea on the blackboard, and then we'll see what we've got. We're not passing judgment on ideas at this point; we're just trying to get a huge list of possibilities and then we'll go from there." Try to solicit ideas from everyone in the room, not just the more outspoken members. If you know that you have a member with good ideas who doesn't like to volunteer, ask that person specifically what his or her thoughts are. Try to keep people from talking over each other or criticizing each other during the brainstorm. Once you have collected a substantial number of ideas, you can advance the discussion by grouping them into categories. You might then open the discussion to the group to evaluate specific proposals, or ask people to e-mail their thoughts after the meeting.

Sometimes people disagree. Those moments of conflict in meetings can be extremely beneficial for the health of your organization. Tough decisions require discussion, but if people are afraid to voice dissent, you may never hear the best idea. Conversely, if discussion devolves into a shouting match, you may find at the end of the meeting that you got nothing done at all. The ability to facilitate discussion—and disagreement—without making enemies is a skill that will be essential to your success as a lawyer, and you should master it sooner rather than later.

A recent law school graduate named Cory, who is particularly adept at guiding meetings where emotions run high, describes his approach:

It takes courage to voice disagreement when you are working in a group. If you're actually willing to speak up, you probably have some strong feeling motivating you. So when I'm leading a group and someone resists something, I try to figure out the motivation underlying the person's words. I ask myself, "What is that person's need?" and then I try to address it.

For example, in my oral advocacy class, my classmates and I were asked to plan and perform a short play. The group chose me as their leader. At one point, a teammate shared her concerns about a segment in which everyone would be dancing. The disagreement had the potential to be divisive because another group member had organized this part of the show and was proud of it. I noticed that the concerned person was using "I" rather than "we" in describing her reservations, which was a change from her earlier comments, so I asked a few questions about what bothered her. As it turned out, her concerns were really about her personal discomfort with movement, and not the direction of the project. When we figured that out, we were able to adjust her role, which reduced her anxiety without disrupting the project as a whole.

As a leader, you should test the ideas being presented, while not discouraging members from offering competing thoughts. When you raise an issue for discussion, be careful not to indicate that you have already made up your mind. If you do, you may shut down conversation from the outset. Your goal is to reach the best outcome for the organization, which means recognizing that the idea you settle on might not be the one you favored at the beginning of the discussion. Try posing questions, rather than making statements.

Your job as a leader requires you to model the kinds of behaviors you want to see practiced during the discussion. Be positive and compliment ideas (and the people who offered them) whenever possible. Your criticism should be constructive, not dismissive or derisive. If you can create an environment where discussion of different ideas is seen as a collaborative search for the best option, as opposed to a conflict where everyone is trying to get his or her way, members generally will be satisfied with the result, even if the idea chosen wasn't their favorite.

During the meeting itself, be aware of group dynamics that might be shutting participants down. Don't let one or two dominant personalities take up all the discussion time. If you run into that problem, control it at the next meeting by making a rule about when people are allowed to talk (for example, during an allotted period of time after officers have presented reports about the matters under discussion), and ask people to raise their hands. Then make a point of calling on people who are reticent first. Do not reflexively call on the first person to raise his hand if this will shut down conversation from other members of the group.

Set the Right Tone

Develop the authority to keep the conversation in a meeting on track. You may find that you have to encourage people to wrap up their thoughts, for example, because a meeting can go off the rails quickly if you allow talkative members to ramble. With practice, you'll find that you can politely but firmly let the person know you need to move on or let other voices be heard. ("Rob, I'm hearing you say that we need a different system for evaluating student note submissions, but before we get any further into how to do that, I'd like to take the temperature of the group to see if we all agree that we need this change. I'd like to call for a vote at this time. . . .") Don't worry that you are going to make someone angry by cutting off conversation about a topic. The rest of the group will respect your leadership and appreciate that you're being thoughtful about the demands on their schedules. If you must table a discussion for another time, ask anyone with unaired viewpoints to submit them to you in an e-mail, which you might then consolidate and share with the group. Keeping the conversation from getting bogged down or hijacked by a handful of talkative people will set the tone for effective meetings going forward.

As the leader you are also responsible for the tone of the discourse. If members are being rude or unprofessional, jump in to ask that they treat each other with respect. If you permit bullying behavior, a meeting can devolve quickly. It can take some courage to stand up to members of your organization who are speaking snidely or behaving aggressively, but the other attendees will appreciate your leadership. Set an example by always speaking professionally and respectfully to others.

Occasionally a leader of a student organization becomes enamored of his own power and engages in bullying himself. Don't fall into this trap, because it will come back to haunt you. For example, don't threaten to punish any of your members for transgressions. If someone fails to turn in a cite check, misses a deadline, or otherwise breaks a promise, responding by threatening to report them to the dean or potential employers will backfire and turn classmates into enemies. If someone isn't living up to his obligations to the organization, simply offer him the chance to make amends or give him the option to withdraw from the club. Anything else will escalate the problem and is likely to hurt you in the long run. Keep in mind that you are in the process of establishing your own professional reputation, so treat your organization's members the way you would want to be treated in return.

Delegate Tasks Effectively

If you want to be an effective leader, you'll soon learn that you can't do everything yourself. Learning to utilize and motivate the talented people you work with will not only help you get more work done, but also will allow you to capitalize on the strengths of others in areas where you might not be as strong. Delegating through effective communication will maximize your organization's production potential, and lead to more engaged members who feel they have a meaningful stake in the organization.

But delegation can be dangerous when it's done haphazardly without clear expectations or goals. If the group member who agrees to do the job does it incorrectly or doesn't do it all, you'll be left to pick up the pieces, often working on a much tighter timetable than if you had simply done it yourself. To avoid this problem, be clear and specific about the task you need completed. Provide a deadline, and make regular checkups on progress if the task is especially lengthy or daunting. Perhaps most importantly, encourage the group member to take ownership over the task. No one wants to spend time on work that is tedious or pointless, so make sure the person to whom you delegate the job understands its importance. Where possible, allow the group member to incorporate his own ideas into the project, and encourage questions and feedback. Incorporating the ideas of multiple people will likely improve the project and bring about better results for your organization.

Expect the Unexpected

The most carefully laid plans can sometimes still go wrong. Even the most responsible members sometimes forget to answer an e-mail, other events may conflict with your meeting times, and guest speakers occasionally cancel at the last minute. When dealing with these unexpected obstacles, it's important to focus on the aspects that are within your control. Anticipate possible challenges and make contingency plans.

For example, if your members aren't responding to e-mail, you might make e-mails shorter and easier to read. You could ask for a response in the subject line instead of hiding the request in the body of the e-mail. For an immediate response, try a phone call or text message. If your regularly scheduled meetings are poorly attended, consider moving them to a day or time when more members can show up. Make sure that the meeting agendas cover information that is important for all members, and consider reducing the number of regular meetings. If a speaker cancels the day before the event, think about whether one of your officers, members, or professors could fill in at the last minute, or reschedule the speech. Remember that you are dealing with busy law students and professors who often have a lot on their plates outside of extracurricular activities, so handle last-minute changes with good grace. Sometimes you'll need to be flexible to get the job done.

But while you should occasionally relax some of your expectations, don't let them fall apart entirely. Members should still be attending regular meetings, responding to e-mails, and doing their fair share of the organization's duties. If members perceive that some students are slacking on their responsibilities, they might follow suit, which could damage the long-term health of the group. The last thing you want is for the organization you care so much about to acquire a reputation as "that club where you don't have to do anything." If that happens, you'll find it more difficult to draw engaged members, and it will be a challenge to accomplish even modest organizational goals. To prevent this, you should be realistic about how much time and effort your members can give, set clear expectations that are in line with these constraints, and apply the same standard to all members equally. As long as you're fair and reasonable, the vast majority of your members will live up to your expectations.

Developing leadership skills takes practice. If you mishandle a conflict or lead a meeting that didn't go well, that doesn't mean you aren't cut out to be a leader. Take the time to evaluate your failures. After each meeting, think about what went well and what didn't, and formulate a plan so the next meeting will be better. Even the very best leaders who seem to run things with ease were not born that way. They had to try, fail, and then pick themselves up and try again. "Natural" leaders may have practiced their opening remarks aloud many times to make them sound polished and smooth. And though they may appear unflappable during a conflict, they probably have moments in private where they express anxiety. But the very best leaders don't appear uncomfortable, because their preparation lends them the confidence to handle the unexpected. These are valuable skills for lawyers to hone, and taking on a leadership role in a student organization offers you a chance to develop them.

Chapter Eight

Interacting with Professors

You may not realize it when they are grilling you on the intricacies of substantive due process, but your professors can be instrumental to your career success. Many desirable legal jobs, like a judicial clerkship or a sought-after fellowship, require applicants to submit letters of recommendation from their professors. Fortunately for you, law school faculty members have valuable contacts at law firms, in the government, and with other employers in the public and private sectors that they will call upon to help a promising student. Some professors have extensive work experience in particular legal fields and can offer helpful insight into the profession as you launch and progress your career. If you want to teach at a law school yourself one day, you'll need the help of the professors who taught you. You very likely considered the strength of the faculty when you chose which law school to attend. Access to that network of faculty (as well as the network of alumni and your fellow classmates) is part of what you're paying for with your tuition dollars. So become part of that network.

But professors aren't going to go to bat for a student they don't know. They might agree to write a reference letter for you, but it won't be particularly special if the professor knows little about you. And if the professor dislikes you or thinks ill of you, he's unlikely to put his reputation at stake for you.

To establish a positive relationship with your professors and build the foundation for a good professional reference, you need to make the most of your interactions with the faculty in and out of the classroom.

Interactions in the Classroom

Students sometimes mistakenly believe they are anonymous in class. Perhaps they're accustomed to extremely large lecture classes from their college days, where attendance is not tracked, and where the professor cannot possibly see all the students sitting in the upper gallery of the lecture hall. So they come to class late; they noisily unwrap their bagel breakfast or an overly fragrant lunch; they text their friends or shop online instead of taking notes. They fall asleep. They laugh at comments e-mailed to them by friends instead of listening to the lecture or contributing to the discussion. They roll their eyes when a classmate they dislike speaks.

Being in a law school class is not like passively watching a television show. The professor can see you. Not only that, but many professors take notes about their students' behavior. Professors typically come to class armed with a seating chart that provides the names of all the students so that he can call on them. When a student is particularly rude, especially to his fellow students, the professor notices. One professor explains:

> This tends to happen when I teach constitutional law. A student may take a position that maybe not everyone in the class loves, and someone volunteers a reply that isn't simply replying to the previous comment on the merits but has an overtone of hostility to it. I really do not appreciate that. There is plenty of hostility out there in the world, but in this environment, it is just not appropriate. What I want [students] to do is to discuss these cases and vigorously express their opinions—really delve into the opinions and dissect them, and explore their strengths and their weaknesses—without rancor. And when [a student is disrespectful], that really annoys me.

So what should you do? Show up on time. Stay awake. Take notes. Resist the urge to surf the Internet. Think about the thousands of dollars that you are spending to be in law school, and take advantage of the time that you're there. And treat your classmates with respect.

Sometimes students who have an earnest desire to learn get off on the wrong foot with a professor by showing bad attention-grabbing habits they might have learned in high school or college. In years past, your teachers may have been very accessible to you, and might have been tolerant of any sort of question that you have. Law school is different. This is the beginning of your professional life, and the actions you take now can affect the reputation you will carry with you into the working world.

Make sure the questions you ask in class exhibit good judgment. If your question is something that will be of general interest or will help move the discussion along, then by all means, raise your hand and ask the question. But if your question is idiosyncratic in nature, or is meant to show off or disparage another classmate, or is something that you could answer for yourself if you were to look at the reading a little more carefully, then don't ask it.

If you miss class, get notes from your classmates. Don't e-mail your professor to ask for his lecture notes. Some professors will provide students with their

PowerPoint teaching slides or other tools, but don't assume that they owe this to you. Most professors believe you should grapple with the material and take your own notes. They will think less of you if you ask them to provide such materials.

Sometimes you'll encounter a professor who seems young or particularly accessible. Don't let that lull you into informality. For example, if you routinely call your older, male professors "Professor," and your younger, female professors by their first names without being invited to do so, you will burn many bridges. Call every professor "Professor." If one prefers being called by her first name, she will let you know.

Be kind to your fellow classmates. Not only will this make your professor like you better, it will also help you make friends in law school. Once you graduate, you'll be astonished to discover that your classmates are not your competition; they are your professional network. They will help you get jobs, find clients, and make connections. While your classmates are unlikely to remember how well you responded to cold calls, they will remember for years a disrespectful comment you made at their expense. Law school can feel intense, but if you resist the urge to succumb to the stress and instead treat classmates nicely, you will lay a good foundation for a strong professional reputation.

Consider enrolling in a small-group class, a clinic, a seminar, or a course that teaches oral presentation skills or trial practice. These classes offer the chance for extensive back-and-forth interactions between faculty and students, and will help you develop a relationship with a professor and hone your public speaking skills at the same time.

Interactions Outside of the Classroom

To cultivate a relationship with a particular professor, you will need to interact with him outside of the classroom. This will likely include both electronic communication and face-to-face meetings. In every interaction, keep in mind Aristotle's lesson of ethos (discussed in Chapter Four): You are more believable if you show good character. Every interaction you have with your professor affects how he views your character. Think through what you want to say before you say it with this in mind.

Electronic Communications

Beware of the informality of e-mail. Students sometimes send professors inappropriate questions, because e-mail makes it so easy to do — for example, "Can you please give me a description of your class?" (when the class description appears on your law school's website), or "Do you have any commercial study aids that you recommend?" (which a professor may interpret as an admission that you don't plan to do the reading). Another strain of inappropriate questions are those that demand the professor's time without being thoughtful about it (e.g., "Could you judge our moot court competition tonight?" or "Could you please write me a letter of recommendation by tomorrow?"), or the e-mail you send in the middle of the night, followed up by a reproachful e-mail if you have not received a reply by the morning. Professors are more likely to respond positively if your question is one you could not have answered on your own, and if you are respectful of the burden that your request might put on the professor. If you're asking for something that will take up the professor's time, be sure to give plenty of notice. Don't expect instantaneous action. If you have a question about material from class, send an e-mail only if the question is short and easily answered. If it requires a complex discussion, go to office hours.

E-mail lives forever. Before you hit the send button, read the e-mail again. Does it capture what you want to say? Could it be misread, with a tone you don't intend? Are you sending the e-mail in frustration or anger? If so, think twice before putting it out there. These cautions especially hold true if you are writing an e-mail about a grade you received. Think about why you're writing that e-mail. Many schools prohibit faculty from changing a grade once it has been submitted, so check your school's policy first to see if it is even worth sending an e-mail. If you are writing because you really want to understand your grade, try a face-to-face conversation instead. If you are writing simply to vent your anger, don't send the e-mail.

"Anonymous" communications aren't always anonymous. For example, even if you think course evaluations are anonymous, law schools will look into evaluations that are particularly vitriolic or make personal attacks on faculty. This could affect your ability to obtain a good letter of recommendation, even from professors other than the one you smeared.

Meeting with Professors

Professors meet with students frequently during their office hours. It's productive to go to your professor's office hours at least once to establish a personal connection with him and to gain a deeper understanding of complex concepts discussed in class. But it is counterproductive to haunt your professor's office if you don't actually have anything to say.

Before you visit during office hours, take a few minutes to plan what you want to ask. You might even want to write out the questions and practice saying them out loud so you appear articulate and confident. But just giving some thought to your question will likely impress the professor, who will appreciate that you are genuinely trying to master the subject but are mindful of using the time well. Kent (from Chapter Three) describes his approach to meeting a professor during office hours:

> I used to avoid office hours because I thought I was bothering the professor. I really never went to see professors in undergrad. And I didn't do it at all my first semester of law school. I think I finally decided that they were willing to answer questions as long as I came with my specific questions ready, and prepared, and was not going to take any more of their time than to answer my specific question. I go in with a prepared list of questions and I have found it very helpful. And not only that, every professor I spoke to was more than happy to answer the questions, so long as I thought about them.

Bring pen and paper with you to write down what your professor tells you. This signals that you're taking the conversation seriously and will remember it after it's over. (Don't ask your professor to provide the paper or pen for you!) Paper is preferable to a laptop because a computer puts a physical barrier between you and the person to whom you are speaking and starts the conversation awkwardly as you boot the computer up (or search for a spare outlet to use because your battery is dying).

Sometimes students take the time to come to office hours to say that a class was particularly helpful, or that they read and liked something that the professor wrote. Professors remember and value these conversations. Some law schools also encourage you to socialize with faculty members by asking them to lunch, and some professors even open their homes to dinners or other social events with students. Take advantage of these opportunities because it can help your teachers get to know you. Realize, though, that if you have been invited to an occasion at a professor's home, the rules of etiquette apply. You should RSVP promptly, and if you say you are going to attend, then you should attend. Don't cancel at the last minute. Even if the law school is footing the bill, the professor has probably gone to some trouble to arrange the event and may even feel nervous about hosting it. If you fail to attend, the professor will notice.

Working for Professors

Another way to connect with professors is to work with them as a research assistant. This can be a terrific job for the summer between your first and second years of law school. Typically it involves helping a professor with research for an article or book that she is writing. You get the chance to master an area of law, and it often requires you to produce a substantial piece of writing that later can be used as a writing sample when applying for other jobs. And over the course of your summer, the professor will get to know you well enough to be able to write a detailed letter of recommendation. (For more thoughts about how to make a summer job successful, see Chapter Ten on communicating at work.) One professor tells this story about his research assistant:

> I taught a small course about the intersection of antitrust and intellectual property law. There was a student in that class who worked with me on his paper, which was a really interesting paper about the Hatch-Waxman Act and its effect on generic pharmaceuticals. He was very interested in the subject, [and] we talked a lot to get him up to speed. He did some really deep research and wrote what I thought was a really excellent paper. I encouraged him to enter it into a contest that the American Bar Association has for antitrust papers, and he won that. This is a guy who went on to do some really, really interesting patent law work. He was very interested in the field, but part of the way he developed his interest — and I think he did himself a huge favor — is he knew that I was also interested in it, and he basically came to me with questions and developed a rapport with me. I really liked the guy, I really liked his paper, he was very easy to work with — he was very pleasant and very sharp. And all of those things together I think really helped him build a background that has helped him have a very successful legal career.

Securing Letters of Recommendation

Once you have performed reasonably well in class, and taken the time to speak to a professor outside of class at least once, then you have laid the foundation to ask her to write you a letter of recommendation. Seek out a professor who has given you a good grade, but also arm her to be able to say something about you as a person. Meet with her or take her to lunch so that she can get to know you. Give her a copy of your resume, transcript, and a brief write-up of what she knows about you and what kind of job or clerkship you are applying for and why. Be sure to ask her for the letter well in advance of any deadlines. Give her the information that she will need to send the letter (such as the address of the person to whom she is writing, the deadline, and so forth). If there are forms that she needs to sign, fill out as much of them as you can for her. Ask for the recommendation in person, and be courteous when you make the request; then follow up in writing with all the information she needs. If the professor appears to hesitate, or says that she can write you a general recommendation but that you were not the strongest person in the class, then beat a hasty retreat and find someone else. A lukewarm recommendation can do more harm than good. Be sure to write a thank-you note and let her know how the job search turns out. Many students never close the loop to tell their recommenders whether or not they got the job. If you let the recommender know, then that person will continue to be a resource for you as you continue forward in your career.

Chapter Nine

Job Interviews

Job interviews are one of the most important tests of your public speaking skills and can set the tone for the launch of your career with a new employer. Other students may tell you scary stories of law firm interviews gone wrong—some of them are so common that they may be more urban legend than real. You may have heard the tale of the student who spoke enthusiastically about working for a particular firm because she just loves New York, only to be told, "You do know that we're in Boston, right?" Or perhaps you've heard the one about the student who called the law firm Shearman & Sterling "Sherwin Williams" throughout the interview. Or—and this one is true—there's the story of a law student who was ill during his callback interview and ended up vomiting in a potted plant in a partner's office.

But that student actually got the job, believe it or not, and you can, too. The trick is to avoid the avoidable mistake (like getting the name of the firm wrong), and to handle unavoidable errors (like a stomach bug) with good grace. This requires a plan. The purpose of this chapter is to offer you one.

First-Round and Callback Interviews: The Basic Structure

Very often, your law school will arrange for legal employers to come to campus to interview students. During this first round of interviews, you will meet with a lawyer or two from a particular law firm (or other legal employer, but I will call them all "law firms" for ease of reference in this chapter) for 20 to 30 minutes. Some law schools permit employers to pre-screen the students that they will interview; if so, the fact that you have been given an interview means you already satisfy their grade requirements for the job, and they are now trying to get a sense of your personality. Students attending law schools that do not allow pre-screening must convince employers that they are qualified. If you do not meet their qualifications on paper (if your grades are too low, for example), then the interviewer may simply engage you in polite conversation to pass the time. You should use the interview to your advantage to convince the employer to give you a second look. Impress the interviewer with other qualities that you can bring to bear, such as your engaging personality or life experience. (More about this to follow.)

If you do well during the on-campus interview, you may be invited for a callback interview. This typically takes place at the law firm, lasts for several hours, and requires meeting with numerous people. The callback also usually includes a formal meal, such as lunch or dinner. If the law firm is located far from your school, the firm typically will pay for your travel expenses, meals, and lodging.

If you are preparing for a callback interview, then the question is not whether you have the skills to do the job. You do. Now they are trying to get a sense of your personality—of whether you're the kind of person they would want to work long hours with, or introduce to a client. Projecting confidence and engaging well during the interview will help you make the case that you're just what they are looking for.

Preparing for the Interview

Preparing for an interview is like preparing for a speech (discussed in Chapter Four): You must know your material well, and you need a theme—a take-home message that you can drive home. Your material is your resume and your legal education so far. Your take-home message should be a theme that highlights the strengths that make you a desirable employee.

Know Your Resume

Your first task is to make sure that you can talk about anything you have included on your resume. Before any interview, pull out your resume and look it over one more time. You will be astonished at the details you have forgotten, and you don't want any part of your resume to take you by surprise. Practice saying a sentence or two aloud about every single item on your resume.

Make sure that your resume draws attention to, rather than distracts employers from, your strengths. Choose details that emphasize your academic abilities, your leadership experience, your ability to work with others, community service, your ethics, and other areas in which you excel.

Find Your Theme

Now take a look at the big picture that your resume describes. Choose a couple of strengths that are consistent with your personal story. Those will be the points to emphasize as a theme during the interview.

For example, when I first interviewed for legal jobs, I felt like I was at a real disadvantage compared to my classmates. Many of my classmates were businesspeople who had corporate experience and were in a joint J.D.-MBA program. Their resumes reflected their interest in corporate work and gave them a coherent story to offer a corporate employer. Other classmates had known from an early age that they wanted to be lawyers, and had majored in pre-law subjects in college and worked as paralegals before coming to law school. They, too, had a compelling story to offer at an interview. I spent my college years directing plays and, before I went to law school, helped run a theater company. The truth was, I wanted a law firm job because I needed health insurance and I wanted to be able to pay down my student loans. These are not the themes that will land you the job.

So I looked my resume over and decided there were two themes I would strike. The first—I was an English major in college and I was on a law journal, so I could demonstrate that I know how to write. The second—I can think on my feet. During interviews, I explained what it meant to direct plays, which requires you to think fast in reaction to what you see actors doing in rehearsal, and to explain clearly and with sensitivity what you want them to change in order to make a scene better. The ability to think on your feet and to articulate your ideas aloud under pressure is useful to litigators, so I would be a valuable asset to an employer.

Think through how each item on your resume supports your theme, or how you could use it to connect back to a point you want to make during the interview. For example, imagine that because you played college basketball, your interviewers seem to want to talk more about your three-point shot than your legal skills. Turn that into a conversation about teamwork, which is something at which you excel. Do you sing in a choir in your free time? Use that experience to illustrate how you are able to collaborate with others and be responsible to other members of a group. *Have an idea about what to say for every single item on your resume.*

Know Why You Want This Job

You should be able to make a case about why you want to work at this particular law firm, in this particular location. Perhaps that answer will be obvious—the law firm concentrates in exactly the kind of work you have been studying, and it's located in your hometown. If the answer is not obvious from your resume, be prepared to explain it. For example, perhaps you want to do the kind of work that is best handled by large law firms, which requires working in an urban environment, but you also enjoy outdoor activities. This could explain why San Francisco is your city of choice.

You may find yourself interviewing at a law firm when you have always imagined yourself as a public interest kind of person, or vice versa. The job interview is not the time to have a crisis of confidence about whether you want the job. You need to figure out why you are there before the interview happens; otherwise, you are wasting your time and the interviewer's as well. Even if the job you are interviewing for is not your dream job, it will have something to offer you. It's a start. Few people stay in the first place they go to work after law school anymore, so there's no need to worry you're closing doors to other opportunities by interviewing for a specific job. Think about the positives of the job, and focus on those during the interview. Save the therapy sessions for outside of the interview room.

Deal with Bad Facts Gracefully

You may have something problematic in your application that you must grapple with during your job search. Perhaps you have a bad grade, or maybe you were unable to find a law-related job after your first year of law school, and so are entering the 2L job hunt with no legal experience. Think of a narrative that addresses this problem and lessens the sting of the bad fact. For example, you might deal with weak first-year grades by focusing on your new studying strategy: "As you can see, I struggled a bit when I first came to law school with figuring out how to distill what I should be learning from the cases I was reading. That's reflected in my first-semester grades. When I got those grades, I reacted by talking to my professors so I could understand where I'd gone wrong, coming up with a new study plan, and working very hard." And there you've laid out a new theme for yourself—you never give up, and you learn from your mistakes. To the extent that you can, focus the conversation on your solution to the problem rather than on the bad grades themselves. It's very possible your interviewer earned some disappointing grades himself in law school, so you may be able to turn that bad fact into a way to make a personal connection.

If you can show that your grades improved in later semesters, point that out. Or if you were able to earn higher marks in seminars or clinics, highlight that and use it as evidence that you excel in situations that allow you to use your interpersonal skills (a good quality in a lawyer). Or perhaps you were able to earn better grades in particular subject areas. If those are the areas in which you hope to practice law one day, then focus on those successes because they show your aptitude for a specific field.

Sometimes poor grades or other bad facts are the result of events beyond your control. Perhaps you lost a family member during the exam period/season, or maybe you were suffering from a medical issue. Excuses are sometimes necessary for bad facts, but offer them with a light touch. Legal recruiters have heard every story in the book, particularly concerning bad grades. If you try to milk the fact that you had a migraine during exams, your story will fall flat if the student who interviewed just before you was struggling with a brain tumor. Practice offering your excuse in under 30 seconds, and then move on to something positive.

Legal employers sometimes become aware of bad facts about a candidate during the vetting process by investigating the candidate on the Internet. Before you start the interviewing process (or even before you start applying to law school), search for references to yourself using Google and other major search engines. Remove any information that you yourself posted online that you would be embarrassed to have an employer see, and un-tag yourself in any embarrassing social media photos. If the negative information is too widespread — for example, if you were arrested in college and there are numerous news stories about it online — consider hiring the services of a company that scrubs personal information from the Internet. You could start using a new variation of your name (using your middle name or initial, for example) if you need to, particularly if your name is common and the negative information actually pertains to someone other than you.

What about when the bad facts are more difficult to spin positively? If you have earned consistently poor grades, have a criminal record, or if an Internet search would reveal a particularly bad result for you, the best you might be able to do is mitigate the damage. There is no perfect job applicant, and many people have these issues and still find employment.

Rather than turning these bad facts into your theme, emphasize the positive characteristics of your application. Maybe you have demonstrated exceptional leadership or community involvement. You may have excellent work experience. The focus of your resume, cover letter, and job interview should be what makes you great, not your past struggles or indiscretions.

If the facts are bad enough, you will at some point need to preempt them with an explanation. It's better to have an employer hear the bad facts from you than for the employer to find out on their own through an Internet search or a background check. Consult with your career services office about whether and when to disclose the negative information. Leading with a bad fact by putting it in a cover letter or explaining it at the start of an interview can sometimes be a mistake because it emphasizes the issue. Very often, the best time to deal with a bad fact is at the scheduling of the callback interview (so if you want to let the law firm know that the John Smith they may have turned up on the Internet is not actually you, mention it to the legal recruiter when you're setting up the callback).

Know the Employer

Spend a little time learning about the law firm interviewing you. Visit the firm's website, read about the firm on resources like chambersandpartners.com, and search for the firm in Google News to see the newsworthy matters that the firm has on its plate right now. And make sure you know the employer's location and name!

Know Your Classes

Anything that appears on your transcript is fair game for a job interview question. So make sure that you can speak about your classes intelligently. This does not mean you have to review all the material as if you were studying for an exam, but you might want to glance over the table of contents in the textbook for the course, or flip through your outline quickly to remind yourself of the most important things you learned. Be ready to explain what class you particularly liked and why.

Know About the World

Particularly during callback interviews, you may have to make intelligent small talk about the day's events. This can be difficult because you are a law student, and very likely you've been buried in the library for months, not checking the latest news. But skim the headlines of the leading news source close to the employer on the day of the interview, or go to Google News and look at the top news articles. There's no need to memorize everything, but you should at least be aware of the latest current events.

Know the Answers to Basic Interview Questions

Be prepared to answer these questions:

- Why do you want to work for (a firm, a nonprofit organization)?
- Why do you want to work for us?
- What are you looking for in a firm?
- Why did you have job X? What did you like about it?

- Why did you go to law school?
- Why this city?
- What class did you like most/least? Why?
- What do you see yourself doing in 10 years?
- What are your strengths/weaknesses?
- What questions do you have for us?

Practice for the Interview

Practice answering the questions you are most likely to be asked. Practice *out loud*. It's not the same exercise to imagine, in the safety of your apartment, how you might answer the question. The first time you formulate your answer out loud, you may sound silly—you may be hesitant, peppering your response with um's and uh's, or striking too arrogant or flattering a tone. Practicing out loud gives you the chance to smooth the delivery, tweak the tone, and figure out the answer that feels the most right to you.

Try practicing with a buddy, preferably another law student (versus, say, your mom, who will find it hard to give you objective advice). Take turns playing the interviewer for one another, and give each other feedback on your answers. Practice the nonverbal parts of the interview as well, such as shaking hands. Here are some things to watch for:

Vocal Tips

Your goal is to speak with confidence, because people can be as affected by the delivery of an answer as they are by its substance. To project confidence:

- **Watch your pace.** Many people speak quickly when nervous. If your interview buddy tells you that you are guilty of this, take a deep breath before the interview in order to calm your nerves. As you exhale, imagine yourself relaxing. During the interview, watch the body language of the person to whom you are speaking. If the person seems confused or tense, take that as a cue that you should slow down. Another clue that you are rattling along too quickly may be that you are out of breath; if you are, take a breath and slow down. It also helps to practice your answers before the interview. The more confident you are, the easier it is to get your nerves under control.

- **Don't speak too quietly.** If you speak softly or mumble, you cannot project authority. This can be particularly frustrating for an older interviewer, who may not be able to hear you. Speak clearly, so that you can be heard. The more confident you sound, the more competent you seem.

- **Watch your pitch.** If you're very nervous, your voice box may freeze up and your voice may sound shrill, which will make you sound insecure. If this happens to you, take a deep breath.

- **Do not use an "upward inflection" if you are making a declarative statement.** If you have the habit of speaking your sentences as if they are questions, practice with your interview buddy until you are able to break the habit. Repetition is required to replace that bad habit with a more confident manner of speaking.

- **Avoid filler sounds, garbage words, or overusing any word.** Practice with your interview buddy until you can answer a question without a single "um," "uh," "like," or "you know." Avoid overusing any word, even if that word is an effective word on its own ("Actually," "Definitely!" "Absolutely!"). If you pepper your answers with words that overstate your point ("It was definitely the best class ever! And I actually loved it! Definitely!"), you will lose credibility.

Mastering Nonverbal Communication

Our body-language signals can be as important as the words we use. Things to think about:

- **Practice shaking hands with your interview buddy.** Shaking hands properly means extending your hand forward with the palm perpendicular to the floor. Use enough pressure so that the recipient of the handshake feels welcomed by you. Don't crush the other person's hand, or offer a wimpy handshake. Also avoid turning your hand—rotating your hand so that your palm faces the floor is a gesture of dominance, while offering a palm face-up is submissive. Through your handshake, you want to communicate confidence and also the fact that you are equals. Stand up when you shake hands at an interview lunch, even if you are female. Normal etiquette says that ladies may stay seated at the table when being introduced, but this isn't a normal situation, and you are not here to be a lady—you are here to be a lawyer. Standing to shake hands shows respect.

- **Sit up straight,** which means pulling your back away from the back of the chair—but not too straight. If you lean back in the chair, you are more likely to slouch. If you are perched too far forward on the edge of the chair and are sitting stiffly, you'll appear nervous. Instead, use posture that shows you're confident and not sloppy. You can watch talk shows that feature conversations (like *The Today Show* or *The View*) to see examples of confident seated postures (usually by the host/interviewer, rather than the guest).

- **Keep your hands resting casually in your lap** or on a folder if you are carrying one, and gesture occasionally when you speak if this is comfortable for you. Avoid hugging yourself or crossing your arms across your chest, which makes you appear ill at ease. A more open posture communicates confidence.

- Once you master the content of your answers, **spend some time on perfecting the mechanics of your delivery.** Start to add hand gestures where appropriate as you practice, and use engaged (but natural) facial expressions.

- **Smile — but not too much.** Smiling a reasonable amount makes you approachable and likeable. Smiling all the time is submissive, a way of asking permission to be a part of the conversation.

- **Don't fidget, play with your clothes, twiddle your hair, or rearrange your jewelry.** Make sure that your suit fits you comfortably so you don't feel compelled to adjust it during your interview. If your jacket is so snug that it's pulling, making you want to wrap your arms in front of yourself to hide the gap, then return the suit and buy a new one, or have it tailored. If your hair is in your eyes, put it up or get a haircut. Men should shave. Get rid of any distracting jewelry. Avoid strong cologne or perfume. These are things your practice buddy can take notes about for you.

- **Look people in the eye.** Your message is more believable if you can hold another person's gaze while delivering it. Again, eye contact is something you can practice with your interview buddy.

What to Wear

Wear a conservative suit to a legal job interview. You may have a more trendy outfit in mind from your previous job — leave it hanging in the closet. In some legal markets (such as certain places in the Deep South), women should wear suits with a skirt, while in other markets (such as New York City), suits with pants are fine for women (although you'll want to check with your career services office to be sure). The suit (for men or for women) should be altered if necessary so that it fits properly. Men should wear conservative ties for similar reasons, as well as dark-colored suits and a white- or blue-collared shirt. Spread-collar shirts are more formal than button-down collars for men, so go with a spread collar to be safe. Your career services office can also advise you on proper attire.

You need to feel comfortable and confident in your suit, so practice wearing it. Think of it as your costume. You want a costume that communicates that you are a confident attorney-to-be. Your clothes should be recently pressed or dry-cleaned and your shoes should be clean and polished. Hang up your clothes after they've been worn or unpacked to avoid wrinkling them. If you're flying to the interview and must wear the suit on the plane, take the jacket off during the flight and hang it up or fold it to avoid wrinkling, and pack an extra shirt, just in case. It's smart to dress nicely on the flight to a job interview—you never know who will be sitting next to you.

Wearing the same outfit to the callback that you wore during the on-campus interview is fine, provided that it is clean and pressed, because if you were dressed properly during the first meeting, the interviewer won't even remember your suit—he'll just remember it was appropriate.

Just as an actor always has several dress rehearsals to become comfortable with a new costume, you also should practice wearing your suit at home so that it feels natural to you. If you feel uncomfortable wearing a suit, that will come through during the interview. If you're used to it, then you won't even have to think about it. You should also become accustomed to the shoes you plan to wear. Break them in before the interview, or all you'll think about on the big day is the blister forming on your foot. You don't want too many "firsts" on interview day. If this is the first day that you are wearing your suit, the first day you are wearing your shoes, the first day you are wearing makeup, the first time you are wearing glasses, or—heaven forbid—the first time you are saying your answers to interview questions out loud, you're setting yourself up for disaster.

When you practice wearing your suit, model the kind of movement you likely will make during the interview. Men should unbutton their suits as they sit. When standing, the top button on a man's two-button suit should be buttoned, and on a man's three-button suit, the middle button or the top two buttons should be buttoned. Practice pulling down your suit jacket (both genders) and smoothing your skirt (women) as you sit. If you sit without adjusting your clothes, you may find that your suit jacket is hunched up around your shoulders, so that you look like a turtle, or that your skirt is riding up too high. Get used to how your interview suit works when you sit down. This is something you might want to practice in front of a mirror.

You will also need some sort of briefcase or tote bag like a lawyer would carry, not a backpack that marks you as a student. If you don't have one, you don't have to break the bank to buy one. Stores like Target sell inexpensive versions of work-appropriate bags that are fine for an interview. The interviewer won't examine your bag closely, but he will notice if your bag is the free backpack that LexisNexis handed out to all the 1Ls. Here's a story from a lawyer with a top-tier law firm in New York who formed a negative impression of an interviewee because of her choice of accessories:

> Once a law student came in to interview at our firm who was carrying her resume in a folder with the Gryffindor House crest on it. I'm a Harry Potter fan too, but that's not something I'd want to lead with in a job interview. It isn't professional. We spent most of the interview talking about Harry Potter because that folder was the first thing that caught my eye, and even though we seemed to be having a friendly conversation, all I kept thinking was, what in the world would she carry if she was going to meet a client? What kind of judgment does that show? And isn't she going to try to tell me something else about herself besides the fact that she likes wizards? Needless to say, she didn't get the job.

Practice carrying your bag or briefcase so that you don't accidentally knock things off people's desks with it. Inside the bag, have multiple copies of all the documents you have already provided to the employer—your resume, your transcript, your references, and a writing sample. If the interviewer has lost a document in the jumble of papers on his desk, you'll be able to smoothly produce a duplicate copy. Also have pen and paper, and an "emergency kit," which might include a comb, a mirror, breath mints, tissues, medicine you need under pressure (aspirin, antacid, and the like), some cash to pay for a cab back to the hotel, and anything else you might require if things go wrong (lipstick, spare hose, hotel address, etc.). Your goal is to be as buttoned-up as possible in advance so you don't have to think about anything during the interview other than the substance of the conversation.

What to Bring to the Interview

- Briefcase
- Resume
- Transcript
- References
- Writing sample
- Pen and paper
- Emergency kit (comb, mirror, breath mints, tissues, medicine you need under pressure)
- Some cash to pay for a cab back to the hotel
- Phone, with the ringer turned off (and don't check for messages during the interview)
- Anything else you might require if things go wrong (lipstick, spare hose, hotel address, etc.)

During the Interview

At its most basic level, an interview is a conversation between you and the interviewer, much like the thousands of other conversations you've had in your life. If you think about what makes a conversation successful, it boils down to a give-and-take between the participants. You should listen to the interviewer's question and answer it (hopefully in a way that reinforces your theme). But this isn't the time to launch into a monologue. If you realize that you have been speaking for five minutes straight, quickly wind up the answer and let the interviewer have a turn.

If you have a passive interviewer, it will be up to you to lead the conversation gracefully. Without seeming impatient or arrogant, direct the conversation toward things that make you an appealing candidate. This is where you will reach for the themes you want to emphasize from your resume. Also think about asking your interviewer questions that will engage him. For example: "I noticed that you've worked here for 10 years. From your perspective as someone who's worked here for a while, what do you believe makes this firm stand out from others?"

If the conversation gets stuck on a topic that isn't helping you advance your case (for example, if the interviewer only wants to talk about your school's prospects for winning the football championship this year), use one of your themes to get the interview back on track. For example: "This may sound a little sentimental, but one of the things I really enjoy about SEC football is being part of a community where people from different walks of life rally around a common goal. That's something I really liked about my job at [former employer] as well ... [continuing on to talk about teamwork at a previous job]."

What about the interviewer who takes 10 minutes to answer each question you ask? Try to be an "active listener," which means responding to the interviewer as you listen. Respond both physically (nod your head, maintain eye contact to show interest) as well as verbally ("That's interesting.") to indicate understanding. You can use verbal interjections to segue into a new topic ("Your story hits on one of the reasons I became interested in this area of the law in the first place...."). You don't want the interview to turn into a power struggle between you and the interviewer, and there certainly are interviewers out there who like to hear themselves talk and will be offended if they perceive you to be interrupting them. But most interviewers have some sense of how to have a conversation, and will let you get a word in edgewise if you indicate politely that you have something to say. If you've noticed that several of your interviews have been dominated by the interviewer, make sure you are not floating passively through the process. Don't limit yourself to responding to questions that the interviewer asks you. Think about the points that you want to be sure to make during the interview, and try (politely) to make them.

Sometimes an interviewer will question you aggressively or ask you something to which you do not know the answer. Your job is to remain unflappable. Very often, the interviewer is more interested in how you handle that kind of situation rather than in whether you know the answer to every question he can dream up. Draw upon the skills you learned in your Socratic Method classes (see Chapters Two and Three) to finesse this part of the interview. Try having your interview buddy take an aggressive tone with you during practice so you can learn to handle the situation with grace. Many students have found it helpful to take an oral advocacy or public speaking class, which will teach you how to appear calm in a stressful situation. You will get better at interviewing the more you do it, and a class that requires you to stand up and speak week after week can help you become more articulate as well. If you really don't know the answer to a question, try reaching for your theme.

Some interviewers may try to assess your attitude toward past work experiences. Stay positive. It's a mistake to take a negative tone during an interview. Avoid any story about how much you dislike a particular professor or past employer. It's also a mistake to laugh at someone else's expense, tell an off-color joke, or appear to put anyone down. If you do, the employer will wonder what nasty thing you will eventually say about him if you come to work for him.

And finally, make a real connection. There is something interesting in every person; find common ground with each interviewer. Strive for a tone that is an authentic version of yourself—except the most polished and polite version of yourself. So if you find yourself out to lunch with some younger lawyers, maybe even people that you know or alumni from your law school, take the opportunity to befriend them. But remember that they are interviewing you, too, so resist the temptation to let your hair down too much by confessing something off-putting (like admitting that you don't really like law school after all). Always stay professional.

Special Issues for Callback Interviews

If you are invited to a callback interview at the firm's office, you will meet people other than those who will be interviewing you, such as administrative assistants, receptionists, and staff from the legal recruiting department. Your interactions with them count. Be polite to everyone, mostly because it's the right thing to do, but also because good manners help you get the job. If you are left to wait outside the office of an important partner and his secretary is sitting there, greet her, introduce yourself, and make small talk if appropriate. It's courteous, plus it will help soothe your nerves.

During a callback interview, ask any person who interviews you for their business card, which you will promptly put into that professional-looking bag you are carrying. The business cards will help you remember names when you write thank-you notes to each interviewer you met. When you have time after the interview, jot a note or two on the back of the business cards about what you and the interviewer discussed so that you can include a reference to that in your message. The thank-you note can be very brief: "Dear John, Thank you for taking the time to meet with me. I was so interested to hear about the work that you do for the National Football League. And it is always a pleasure to meet a fellow Packers fan. I am impressed by your law firm and appreciate being considered for a summer associate position. I hope that I have the chance to see you again in the future. Sincerely, Mary Brown." Type it on plain, white business stationery and send it out promptly after the interview is over.

The callback interview often involves being treated to an upscale lunch with a group of lawyers from the firm. Keep in mind that the point of the lunch is to get the job, not to eat the food. Order things that are easy to eat, so you can focus on the conversation rather than on how to keep linguini with marinara sauce from splattering all over your suit. Choose something that is easy to clean up if it does spill on you (again, a reason to avoid the marinara sauce). Choose something mid-priced, rather than the most expensive thing on the menu. Many lawyers will order an appetizer, entrée and dessert, but as budgets have tightened, some have given up this practice. If you aren't sure whether to order three courses or just an entrée, follow the lead of the others at the table. If the server comes to you first, simply say, "I just need one more minute. Would you come back to me?" and see what others do. Remember that your bread plate is the one on your left, and your water glass is the one on your right. (A trick for remembering this—put both hands in a "thumbs-up" position, and turn them so that your palms are facing up. Your left hand looks like a b, which stands for bread plate. Your right hand looks like a d, which stands for drink.) Put your napkin in your lap, don't eat until everyone has been served, and make an effort to carry on an engaging conversation. Don't drink alcohol during an interview lunch. Alcohol is not your friend.

Never, under any circumstances, answer your phone or check your e-mail during an interview. This includes the interview lunch. Turn all those devices off and focus on the task at hand—getting the job.

The callback interview and the lunch are a time for you and the potential employer to get to know each other and see if your personalities click. You should demonstrate that you can handle any social situation you might have to engage in with a client, because that's part of the job. Your grades will only get you through the screening interview—your ability to hold a decent conversation and make friends will land you the offer.

How to Network

Very often, people get jobs because they know someone who knows someone who is hiring. Many law students express squeamishness about using connections, mistakenly believing that it is somehow nobler to acquire a job from a total stranger, purely on the strength of your transcript. This is nonsense.

Two of the best jobs I have had in my legal career—working at the Department of Justice and becoming a professor at the University of Virginia School of Law—were the direct result of a friendly colleague going to bat for me. In both cases, someone who knew me was willing to walk my resume into the office of the person in charge and put in a good word for me. In a sea of highly qualified candidates, and particularly during a time of economic downturn, you need that personal touch to get noticed. It can make all the difference.

Be willing to network. Let people know that you are looking for employment. If your father's golf buddy offers to introduce you to his lawyer, accept the introduction. You never know what fantastic opportunity awaits.

One student I interviewed, David, found himself affected by tough economic times that had impacted legal hiring—the law firm where he worked during the summer following his second year did not extend permanent job offers to many of its summer associates, including him. He tried the usual course of interviewing on campus during his third year, to no avail. But just when he began to despair, his willingness to make a personal connection ultimately landed him a pretty interesting job. He tells this story:

> The job search is really tough if you do not get a permanent offer from your second summer job. That's how it's supposed to work out. If it doesn't, then you're thrown out into a job market as a 3L where firms basically have their hiring needs filled already from your class and are looking at 2Ls instead.
>
> Near the end of my last year of law school, I hadn't found anything. Then Tucker Carlson [a well-known political news commentator] came to UVA. He was invited by one of the student groups to speak about the 2012 election cycle. On a whim, I decided to go. Tucker gave his speech, and I asked the last question during the Q&A session. And he liked the question. After the talk was over, I went up and talked to him. I introduced myself, reminded him of my question, and ended up talking to him about the fact that we're both Episcopalian and going to be living in D.C. He

asked, "Well, what will you be doing in D.C.?" And I told him I didn't really know because I didn't have a job, but I figured with a law degree, D.C.'s a pretty good place to be. And he says, "Well, you know, if you don't have anything else to do, would you consider being a reporter—come on and work for me? Would you be interested?" So I'm going to be writing on legal and political issues for Tucker Carlson's website, *The Daily Caller.*

David says that when he was a first-year law student, he probably would not have approached Tucker Carlson at all. But by the time he was a 3L, he'd become more outspoken because of his experiences in law school classes. In particular, he signed up for several courses that required substantial class participation, and the more he did it, the more confident he became in his speaking ability.

Be confident. Be friendly. Be yourself at your best. Make connections. Figure out why you are a good fit for a job and tell the employer. Your verbal persuasion skills can make all the difference.

Chapter Ten

Communicating on the Job

For many students, law school is more than just the training ground for a new career. It's also a place of transition, where you are nudged out of a familiar academic environment to take your place as a member of the Bar. To make your own transition successfully, you should practice and learn to excel at communicating with those who hold power in the world you seek to enter. You have to learn to speak their language.

During the summer, law students typically work for law firms or other kinds of legal service employers to gain experience and earn money to pay for school. At a law firm, this summer job can act as a sort of lengthy interview, and you should approach it that way. Summer associates who perform well are often offered permanent positions pending graduation from law school. The quality of your written work certainly plays an important role in whether you will land that offer, but very frequently, your verbal communication skills are even more critical. You and your fellow summer associates may be equally qualified, and produce equally excellent work. The way to stand out is to connect with the attorneys around you.

Your first job at a law firm or with another legal industry employer may also be the first time you interact regularly with people of a different generation or background than you (other than your parents and teachers, who were there to support and guide you). Suddenly your role shifts—as a summer associate or entry-level attorney, you have been hired to support the more-senior lawyers, and even though you are (or will be) a lawyer yourself, their priorities and expectations trump yours. It can be helpful to understand what senior colleagues expect from you, and how your communication style can affect the impression that you make.

Electronic Communications

As a student, your electronic communications—e-mail, texts, and chat—are typically informal, fired off quickly without a second glance, and sometimes employ abbreviations and emoticons.

Once you begin working, you should start thinking of your e-mails as business communications. Write complete sentences, check spelling, and use the same level of formality you would use in a business letter—"Dear John," rather than "Hi, there." Even if the partner to whom you are writing fires off incoherent e-mails to you from his mobile phone, don't respond in kind. Play it safe and make sure that your e-mails always look professional. Very often, the lawyers judging your work came of age when business communications required polished letters or formal memos. Even if they don't use a formal tone when communicating with you, they may judge your e-mails by the standards that were applied to them when they were junior lawyers.

But also consider whether e-mail is even the best way to communicate in a particular situation. If the topic that you are raising is complex, it might be better suited to a face-to-face conversation, which also permits you the chance to really get to know your colleagues and make a personal connection with them. Partners may grow impatient if you expect them to write a long explanation about something. Think about the demands on their time, and whether it would be easier for them to explain something to you in person.

E-mail also can be forwarded, so don't put anything in an e-mail that would embarrass you if it were to be disseminated widely. Here's an example *The Boston Globe* reported on in February 2006 under the headline, "Two E-mailers Get Testy, and Hundreds Read Every Word." According to the story, a recent law school graduate had agreed to work for a criminal defense firm, but changed her mind. She sent the lawyer an e-mail that said, "The pay you are offering would neither fulfill me nor support the lifestyle I am living." The lawyer replied that the associate's decision to inform him of this via e-mail rather than in person "smacks of immaturity and is quite unprofessional." He also noted that he had spent some money in anticipation of her arrival on such things as business cards and stationery. Her curt retort: "A real lawyer would have put the contract into writing and not exercised any such reliance until he did so." His: "Thank you for the refresher course on contracts. This is not a bar exam question. You need to realize that this is a very small legal community, especially the criminal defense bar. Do you really want to start pissing off more experienced lawyers at this early stage of your career?" Her final three-word response: "bla bla bla." The lawyer forwarded the exchange to a colleague, who sent it to another, and then it went viral. You can imagine the damage this did to the recent graduate's reputation. The lesson: Be careful what you put in an e-mail.

Once you work in a legal setting, you also have to take into account attorney-client privilege—this means you can't forward an e-mail that contains privileged information to friends or family, for example. E-mails are sometimes discoverable in a lawsuit, so exercise good judgment about what you commit to writing. If you have a thought that could damage a client, discuss it in person rather than writing about it.

E-mail can also take on a tone that you did not intend. *If you're angry or upset when you write an e-mail, do not hit the send button.* Take a deep breath and let some time pass. Once you are calm, go speak to the intended recipient in person. Very often, people will say things in e-mails that they would never actually say to someone's face. If a situation is growing tense, you can defuse it better with an in-person conversation than with an electronic volley of words.

In-Person Meetings

Even if you've mastered the art of effective electronic communications, resist the temptation to rely on them too heavily. It can seem easier to fire off an e-mail to a colleague, but if you do that, you miss the chance to make a connection. In fact, one common complaint that older lawyers make about younger attorneys is that they are so attached to their gadgets and computers that they don't know how to talk to other people. This offers you a great opportunity to stand out by being the one who's not afraid of face-to-face conversation.

If you have completed an assignment for a partner, go see the partner in person rather than simply submitting the assignment to him. Think of a few points to make about the memo you've just written, practice saying them so that you have some sense of how to express them, then go down the hall to see if the partner is available for a few minutes to meet and talk about the work. (If it's not a good time, ask him if he has time later or perhaps ask him to lunch.) Then distill your findings for him and point out any areas of follow-up inquiry that you think the assignment might raise. Articulating your findings aloud helps the partner understand the memo and gives you a chance to show off what you know. Thinking strategically about any follow-up work that your memo might generate shows the partner that you are creative and have taken an interest in the issues at hand.

When you meet face to face, consider bringing a pen and paper in addition to (or maybe even instead of) a laptop. Taking notes at a meeting with a supervisor or client signals that you are taking their time seriously and that you won't have to ask them to repeat something later. But sometimes taking notes on a laptop separates you from the person you are speaking with. A pad of paper can be a more low-key way to take notes and keep you connected with the other people in the room.

You should also bring supporting information with you to a meeting—the memo you wrote, the cases you cited, the document you are discussing, etc. Develop a filing system so that you have a folder for every matter you're work-ing on with the important documents in it, organized so you can find them quickly. If you asked for the meeting, then think through what the partner might want to see or ask about in detail, and bring those documents along, even if nobody asked you to. Bring a second copy that you could leave with the partner if he asks, with the important information flagged for him. If you were called into the meeting on short notice, then a good filing system will prove quite valuable to you. Grab the relevant file or folder and go. You will impress your colleagues if you are able to quickly produce the information they need, rather than having to shuffle through your materials or race back to your office to find it.

It might not be appropriate for you to chime in during a team meeting if you are inexperienced and the stakes are high, such as if the client or opposing counsel are present. But if the meeting is more akin to a brainstorming session, and you have an idea to contribute, then you should offer it. It can help if you think through what you want to say before the meeting starts and practice say-ing it out loud a few times in the privacy of your office. It's often easier to jump in at the start of a meeting, so if you know you have something to offer, con-sider doing so early on rather than waiting until things wrap up. If you're not sure what to say, then take the opposite approach—listen to the rest of the conversation, and offer something at the end, when you have solidified your thoughts.

If you are asked to make a presentation to a practice group or your fellow summer associates, take that opportunity to showcase your verbal skills. Re-view Chapter Four for instructions about how to make a formal verbal pres-entation.

Asking Questions

Always ask appropriate questions. For example, any time you receive an as-signment, ask what the deadline is, who the client is (and the billing number), what form the assignment should take (A memo? An e-mail?), and whether there is a limit to the amount of time that you should spend on the project. Write down the answers to these questions, because you will look foolish if you have to ask them again.

Once you begin working on the project, you will have additional questions. Follow the same procedure that you would in meeting with a professor — think about what you want to ask, don't ask the question to which you could easily find the answer yourself, and take the time to formulate how to ask what you need to know. Then go ask with confidence and as articulately as possible.

The flip side to the "always ask appropriate questions" rule is to avoid asking inappropriate questions. For example, think twice about peppering a partner or senior associate with questions throughout the day. You may have been encouraged to ask lots of questions in school, and you may think that's a way to show you are interested and engaged. It's not, if the questions that you are asking are ones that you can answer yourself. Asking too many questions indicates a lack of judgment on your part, and communicates that you're not respecting how valuable the attorney's time is. So before you send that e-mail with the quick question, think it through. Are you asking the right person — could a senior associate answer, instead of the partner, whose time is more limited? Is it something that you can answer yourself with a little effort? Have you already asked a lot of other questions? Compile all your questions into one e-mail, rather than peppering your supervisor with a barrage of e-mails as questions occur to you throughout the day.

Offering solutions, rather than simply asking questions, is the mark of a good lawyer. If you're faced with a problem that requires a judgment call, try forming and explaining your opinion on the issue rather than simply punting the question to your boss. When I supervised the work of law students and new attorneys during my time at a law firm, I noticed law students would turn in memos saying, "This raises a lot of questions." Lawyers would turn in memos saying, "This raises a lot of questions, and here are some possible answers."

Professional Behavior

In addition to electronic and verbal communications, you can make an impression on your law firm colleagues through a range of behaviors. As one legal recruiter explained, "You don't lose the job during the interview itself. You lose it in the cracks in between." Your success as a summer associate rests not just on the work that you do, but also on the moments in between assignments. The following suggestions will help cement your reputation as a competent, reliable professional.

Dress Professionally

Dress professionally, which typically means some level of formality (a suit and nice shoes, for example). If in doubt, dress conservatively. Some lawyers may consider any sort of bare skin to be inappropriate, which may require you to wear hose with skirts, or to eschew bare arms. It's generally better to be the most nicely dressed person in the room than to be the only one in business-casual clothes when everyone else is wearing a suit. Some lawyers keep an extra suit in the office at all times, in case they find themselves unexpectedly summoned to see a client. Make sure that your clothes are in good repair and free of dirt and missing buttons. If you are unsure about whether something is appropriate to wear, don't wear it.

Turn in Your Assignments on Time

If you realize you need more time to finish an assignment, tell the partner right away and offer to give him an oral report on the work that you have been able to complete.

Show Up to Work on Time and Work for the Entire Workday

Some law firms permit you to work remotely on occasion. Don't do it during your first summer. This is the time to show the attorneys you are diligent and dedicated. You won't deliver that impression if you're not in your office when your colleagues are. Even after you land the job full-time, spend the first year establishing your good reputation before you take advantage of alternative work arrangements. More-senior lawyers may see your absence from the office as a signal that you aren't committed to the job, so spend your first year showing that you are. But once you have established your good reputation, and have learned how to work remotely without negatively impacting other members of your team, colleagues will focus more on your work than on where you are working.

Take Any Legal Training Classes the Employer Offers

Many law firms offer classes to summer associates that train you to take depositions, draft contracts, or engage in mock trials. Take advantage of these opportunities. They are generally quite rewarding, and the firm has invested a great deal of money to make the programs available to you. If you jump in with both feet and try to get something out of the training, the lawyers who organized it will remember you positively. Training classes are also a great way for you to show off your skills, or at least your willingness to learn something new. Don't complain about training classes (or any program that your firm has organized for you) — someone has devoted time and resources to make it happen, and you risk offending that person if you bad-mouth the offering.

Beware of Multitasking

If you are on a conference call or at a meeting, pay attention. Do not work on other projects at the same time, or check your e-mail. Stay engaged with the project at hand. One law firm partner had this to say about the subject:

> Supervising new attorneys can be so frustrating. I had this one woman who worked for me who would send out e-mails about one case while we were on conference calls with a client from another case — and she would copy me on the e-mails, which made it obvious that she was doing it! So I knew she was not properly listening to the call.

Social Events

You may be invited to firm cocktail parties or dinner parties at partners' houses. These events are not optional. They are designed to help you forge personal connections with colleagues, and you should take advantage of them. The same rules apply here as at parties thrown by your professors — you cannot bail at the last minute, because you will offend the host if you do. Even if the law firm is paying for the event, the host still went to some trouble and may take it personally if you don't attend.

If you're not an extroverted person, then prepare yourself before you go. Look over the names of the people who are likely to be there, and think of something to ask various lawyers whom you are likely to encounter. An easy question is, "What are you working on lately?" People enjoy talking about themselves, so any open-ended question that lets a lawyer ramble about his work is likely to engage that person's attention.

Force yourself to speak to at least one new person at each social occasion. Don't hide in the corner; go up to people and introduce yourself as a summer associate. The other lawyers are there to meet you, so they are likely to appreciate it if you make that job easier for them. If you are truly terrified, look around the room for any other person standing by himself. That person is even more terrified than you are. Go talk to him.

Look people in the eye when you talk to them, and be sure to smile. *Do not scan the room with your eyes to see if there's anyone better that you can talk to.*

People notice that, and they don't forget it. If you are talking to someone, focus your whole attention on that person. Notice physical cues—if the person seems to want to end the conversation, take the hint. Or if you are the person who would like to escape the conversation, end it by bringing another person into the group ("Have you met Megan? She's a from NYU Law School."), turning to the food/drink ("Doesn't that buffet look great? Should we check it out?"/"Please excuse me—I'd like to get a drink."), or any other gracious exit line ("It's been so nice to meet you. Good luck with that interesting case!").

Students sometimes find it difficult to balance the work of their summer associate jobs with social events they also need to attend. What if that partner you've been trying to strike up a conversation with asks you to play golf, but you are also tasked with a ton of work that is due by the end of the week? Although the timing might not be ideal, you should play golf with the partner and stay late at the office the rest of the week to finish the work. When you are trying to obtain a permanent position with the firm, one-on-one time with an influential partner is as good as any chance you are likely to get to make a connection and stand apart from other associates. Don't waste that opportunity, or even worse, make the partner feel like you are blowing him off. Although you should always be sure to get your work done, most firms don't expect their summer associates to spend all of their time at the office—but they will expect you to show commitment to the firm and interest in the people that work there.

A final caution: Behave yourself. Some lawyers behave badly at their firm's social functions. The job is full of pressure and the hours can be long, so some lawyers will drink too much or spend the firm's money lavishly in order to reward themselves. Some lawyers have affairs with one another. Some say things that they shouldn't. Don't follow their example. Here's a story from a lawyer at a large Washington, D.C. law firm about a memorable summer associate:

> The law firm had a scavenger hunt one summer as a get-to-know-you event for summer associates and lawyers. They rented a fleet of limousines and drove us all around the city while we tried to find various things on lists they'd given us. The idea was to be creative and see the city a little (so the list might ask you to get a picture in front of the Washington Monument or something like that). But you weren't really supposed to go buy the things; you were supposed to scavenge them. One of the things on our list was a movie ticket stub, so when we went by a movie theater, this one summer associate grabbed my purse, ran up to the ticket window, and used *my* money to buy a ticket to a show. Then she ripped the ticket in half so it could be our ticket stub. That may sound like a little thing, but it really turned me off because it was cheating and also misusing what

she assumed was the firm's money, but it actually was my money because there was no way I could ask to be reimbursed for that. So later in the summer she was assigned to work for me, and I was much more critical of her memo than I think I would have been if I hadn't already disliked her. I thought of her as a cheater, so I took the time to read all the sources she cited in her memo, and sure enough, I found plenty of places where she hadn't really cited cases accurately but instead was just trying to get the memo to come out the way our client wanted. She didn't get a permanent offer at the firm.

Even when everyone seems to be cutting loose, keep in mind that everything you do counts toward your professional reputation, and there's at least one person in the room who is stone-cold sober and watching. Show good judgment.

Epilogue

Being a lawyer is more than simply a job. It's a profession that offers the opportunity to do some real good in the world. If you take your legal education seriously, you can learn how to right wrongs, champion causes, and defend people who cannot defend themselves. The law can be a powerful instrument of change. Hold tight to the idealism and aspirations that brought you to law school in the first place.

The law is also a locus of power. Lawyers are uniquely positioned to take actions that have far-reaching consequences in our society through the practice of law, politics, or through the myriad non-legal careers that many law school graduates fashion for themselves. What you say can impact the world for good — or for ill. Think about Aristotle's lesson of ethos, and hold yourself to the highest ethical standard. Don't use your skills of verbal persuasion to pull the wool over people's eyes. Use them to bring the truth to light.

Finally, even when you feel overwhelmed by the enormity of the workload, the high stakes of the case on which you are working, or the contentiousness of the adversarial system, realize that you can do this. Have faith in your own abilities and intuitions. Remember the lesson that law school teaches again and again: Often, there is no one "right" answer. Instead, there are possibilities. The more you speak up, the better a lawyer you will become, and the more likely you are to achieve your goals. It's well worth the effort to learn how to raise your voice, because that's how you will empower yourself, and how you will change the world.

Appendix of Cases and Rules

From Chapter One:

212 So. 2d 906 (1968)
District Court of Appeal of Florida. Second District.

Audrey E. VOKES, Appellant,

v.

ARTHUR MURRAY, INC., a Corporation, J.P. Davenport, d/b/a Arthur Murray School of Dancing, Appellees.

Record No. 67-476.
July 31, 1968.

PIERCE, Judge.

This is an appeal by Audrey E. Vokes, plaintiff below, from a final order dismissing with prejudice, for failure to state a cause of action, her fourth amended complaint, hereinafter referred to as plaintiff's complaint.

Defendant Arthur Murray, Inc., a corporation, authorizes the operation throughout the nation of dancing schools under the name of "Arthur Murray School of Dancing" through local franchised operators, one of whom was defendant J.P. Davenport whose dancing establishment was in Clearwater.

Plaintiff Mrs. Audrey E. Vokes, a widow of 51 years and without family, had a yen to be "an accomplished dancer" with the hopes of finding "new interest in life." So, on February 10, 1961, a dubious fate, with the assist of a motivated acquaintance, procured her to attend a "dance party" at Davenport's "School of Dancing" where she whiled away the pleasant hours, sometimes in a private room, absorbing his accomplished sales technique, during which her grace and poise were elaborated upon and her rosy future as "an excellent dancer" was painted for her in vivid and glowing colors. As an incident to this interlude, he sold her eight 1/2-hour dance lessons to be utilized within one calendar month therefrom, for the sum of $14.50 cash in hand paid, obviously a baited "come-on."

Thus she embarked upon an almost endless pursuit of the terpsichorean art during which, over a period of less than sixteen months, she was sold fourteen "dance courses" totaling in the aggregate 2,302 hours of dancing lessons for a total cash outlay of $31,090.45, all at Davenport's dance emporium. All of these fourteen courses were evidenced by execution of a written "Enrollment Agreement—Arthur Murray's School of Dancing" with the addendum in heavy black print, "No one will be informed that you are taking dancing lessons. Your relations with us are held in strict confidence," setting forth the number of "dancing lessons" and the "lessons in rhythm sessions" currently sold to her from time to time, and always of course accompanied by payment of cash of the realm.

These dance lesson contracts and the monetary consideration therefor of over $31,000 were procured from her by means and methods of Davenport and his associates which went beyond the unsavory, yet legally permissible, perimeter of "sales puffing" and intruded well into the forbidden area of undue influence, the suggestion of falsehood, the suppression of truth, and the free exercise of rational judgment, if what plaintiff alleged in her complaint was true. From the time of her first contact with the dancing school in February, 1961, she was influenced unwittingly by a constant and continuous barrage of flattery, false praise, excessive compliments, and panegyric encomiums, to such extent that it would be not only inequitable, but unconscionable, for a Court exercising inherent chancery power to allow such contracts to stand.

She was incessantly subjected to overreaching blandishment and cajolery. She was assured she had "grace and poise"; that she was "rapidly improving and developing in her dancing skill"; that the additional lessons would "make her a beautiful dancer, capable of dancing with the most accomplished dancers"; that she was "rapidly progressing in the development of her dancing skill and gracefulness," etc., etc. She was given "dance aptitude tests" for the ostensible purpose of "determining" the number of remaining hours of instructions needed by her from time to time.

At one point she was sold 545 additional hours of dancing lessons to be entitled to award of the "Bronze Medal" signifying that she had reached "the Bronze Standard," a supposed designation of dance achievement by students of Arthur Murray, Inc.

Later she was sold an additional 926 hours in order to gain the "Silver Medal," indicating she had reached "the Silver Standard," at a cost of $12,501.35.

At one point, while she still had to her credit about 900 unused hours of instructions, she was induced to purchase an additional 24 hours of lessons to participate in a trip to Miami at her own expense, where she would be "given the opportunity to dance with members of the Miami Studio."

She was induced at another point to purchase an additional 126 hours of lessons in order to be not only eligible for the Miami trip but also to become "a life member of the Arthur Murray Studio," carrying with it certain dubious emoluments, at a further cost of $1,732.30.

At another point, while she still had over 1,000 unused hours of instruction she was induced to buy 151 additional hours at a cost of $2,049.00 to be eligible for a "Student Trip to Trinidad," at her own expense as she later learned.

Also, when she still had 1,100 unused hours to her credit, she was prevailed upon to purchase an additional 347 hours at a cost of $4,235.74, to qualify her to receive a "Gold Medal" for achievement, indicating she had advanced to "the Gold Standard."

On another occasion, while she still had over 1,200 unused hours, she was induced to buy an additional 175 hours of instruction at a cost of $2,472.75 to be eligible "to take a trip to Mexico."

Finally, sandwiched in between other lesser sales promotions, she was influenced to buy an additional 481 hours of instruction at a cost of $6,523.81 in order to "be classified as a Gold Bar Member, the ultimate achievement of the dancing studio."

All the foregoing sales promotions, illustrative of the entire fourteen separate contracts, were procured by defendant Davenport and Arthur Murray, Inc., by false representations to her that she was improving in her dancing ability, that she had excellent potential, that she was responding to instructions in dancing grace, and that they were developing her into a beautiful dancer, whereas in truth and in fact she did not develop in her dancing ability, she had no "dance aptitude," and in fact had difficulty in "hearing the musical beat." The complaint alleged that such representations to her "were in fact false and known by the defendant to be false and contrary to the plaintiff's true ability, the truth of plaintiff's ability being fully known to the defendants, but withheld from the plaintiff for the sole and specific intent to deceive and defraud the plaintiff and to induce her in the purchasing of additional hours of dance lessons." It was averred that the lessons were sold to her "in total disregard to the true physical, rhythm, and mental ability of the plaintiff." In other words, while she first exulted that she was entering the "spring of her life," she finally was awakened to the fact there was "spring" neither in her life nor in her feet.

The complaint prayed that the Court decree the dance contracts to be null and void and to be cancelled, that an accounting be had, and judgment entered against the defendants "for that portion of the $31,090.45 not charged against specific hours of instruction given to the plaintiff." The Court held the complaint not to state a cause of action and dismissed it with prejudice. We disagree and reverse.

The material allegations of the complaint must, of course, be accepted as true for the purpose of testing its legal sufficiency. Defendants contend that contracts can only be rescinded for fraud or misrepresentation when the alleged misrepresentation is as to a material fact, rather than an opinion, prediction or expectation, and that the statements and representations set forth at length in the complaint were in the category of "trade puffing," within its legal orbit.

It is true that "generally a misrepresentation, to be actionable, must be one of fact rather than of opinion." *Tonkovich v. South Florida Citrus Industries, Inc.,* Fla.App. 1966, 185 So.2d 710; *Kutner v. Kalish,* Fla.App. 1965, 173 So.2d 763. But this rule has significant qualifications, applicable here. It does not apply where there is a fiduciary relationship between the parties, or where there has been some artifice or trick employed by the representor, or where the parties do not in general deal at "arm's length" as we understand the phrase, or where the representee does not have equal opportunity to become apprised of the truth or falsity of the fact represented. 14 Fla.Jur. Fraud and Deceit, § 28; *Kitchen v. Long,* 1914, 67 Fla. 72, 64 So. 429. As stated by Judge Allen of this Court in *Ramel v. Chasebrook Construction Company,* Fla. App. 1961, 135 So. 2d 876:

> "A statement of a party having superior knowledge may be regarded as a statement of fact although it would be considered as opinion if the parties were dealing on equal terms."

It could be reasonably supposed here that defendants had "superior knowledge" as to whether plaintiff had "dance potential" and as to whether she was noticeably improving in the art of terpsichore. And it would be a reasonable inference from the undenied averments of the complaint that the flowery eulogiums heaped upon her by defendants as a prelude to her contracting for 1,944 additional hours of instruction in order to attain the rank of the Bronze Standard, thence to the bracket of the Silver Standard, thence to the class of the Gold Bar Standard, and finally to the crowning plateau of a Life Member of the Studio, proceeded as much or more from the urge to "ring the cash register" as from any honest or realistic appraisal of her dancing prowess or a factual representation of her progress.

Even in contractual situations where a party to a transaction owes no duty to disclose facts within his knowledge or to answer inquiries respecting such facts, the law is if he undertakes to do so he must disclose the *whole truth*. *Ramel v. Chasebrook Construction Company, supra; Beagle v. Bagwell*, Fla. App. 1964, 169 So. 2d 43. From the face of the complaint, it should have been reasonably apparent to defendants that her vast outlay of cash for the many hundreds of additional hours of instruction was not justified by her slow and awkward progress, which she would have been made well aware of if they had spoken the "whole truth."

In *Hirschman v. Hodges*, etc., 1910, 59 Fla. 517, 51 So. 550, it was said that — "what is plainly injurious to good faith ought to be considered as a fraud sufficient to impeach a contract," and that an improvident agreement may be avoided — "because of surprise, or mistake, *want of freedom, undue influence, the suggestion of falsehood, or the suppression of truth*." (Emphasis supplied.)

We repeat that where parties are dealing on a contractual basis at arm's length with no inequities or inherently unfair practices employed, the Courts will in general "leave the parties where they find themselves." But in the case sub judice, from the allegations of the unanswered complaint, we cannot say that enough of the accompanying ingredients, as mentioned in the foregoing authorities, were not present which otherwise would have barred the equitable arm of the Court to her. In our view, from the showing made in her complaint, plaintiff is entitled to her day in Court.

It accordingly follows that the order dismissing plaintiff's last amended complaint with prejudice should be and is reversed.

Reversed.

LILES, C.J., and MANN, J., concur.

From Chapter Two:

196 Va. 493
Supreme Court of Appeals of Virginia

W. O. LUCY and J. C. LUCY
v.
A. H. ZEHMER and Ida S. ZEHMER.

Record No. 4272.
November 22, 1954.

BUCHANAN, J., delivered the opinion of the court.

This suit was instituted by W. O. Lucy and J. C. Lucy, complainants, against A. H. Zehmer and Ida S. Zehmer, his wife, defendants, to have specific performance of a contract by which it was alleged the Zehmers had sold to W. O. Lucy a tract of land owned by A. H. Zehmer in Dinwiddie County containing 471.6 acres, more or less, known as the Ferguson farm, for $50,000. J. C. Lucy, the other complainant, is a brother of W. O. Lucy, to whom W. O. Lucy transferred a half interest in his alleged purchase.

The instrument sought to be enforced was written by A. H. Zehmer on December 20, 1952, in these words: "We hereby agree to sell to W. O. Lucy the Ferguson Farm complete for $50,000.00, title satisfactory to buyer," and signed by the defendants, A. H. Zehmer and Ida S. Zehmer.

The answer of A. H. Zehmer admitted that at the time mentioned W. O. Lucy offered him $50,000 cash for the farm, but that he, Zehmer, considered that the offer was made in jest; that so thinking, and both he and Lucy having had several drinks, he wrote out "the memorandum" quoted above and induced his wife to sign it; that he did not deliver the memorandum to Lucy, but that Lucy picked it up, read it, put it in his pocket, attempted to offer Zehmer $5 to bind the bargain, which Zehmer refused to accept, and realizing for the first time that Lucy was serious, Zehmer assured him that he had no intention of selling the farm and that the whole matter was a joke. Lucy left the premises insisting that he had purchased the farm.

Depositions were taken and the decree appealed from was entered holding that the complainants had failed to establish their right to specific performance, and dismissing their bill. The assignment of error is to this action of the court.

W. O. Lucy, a lumberman and farmer, thus testified in substance: He had known Zehmer for fifteen or twenty years and had been familiar with the Ferguson farm for ten years. Seven or eight years ago he had offered Zehmer $20,000 for the farm which Zehmer had accepted, but the agreement was verbal and Zehmer backed out. On the night of December 20, 1952, around eight o'clock, he took an employee to McKenney, where Zehmer lived and operated a restaurant, filling station and motor court. While there he decided to see Zehmer and again try to buy the Ferguson farm. He entered the restaurant and talked to Mrs. Zehmer until Zehmer came in. He asked Zehmer if he had sold the Ferguson farm. Zehmer replied that he had not. Lucy said, "I bet you wouldn't take $50,000.00 for that place." Zehmer replied, "Yes, I would too; you wouldn't give fifty." Lucy said he would and told Zehmer to write up an agreement to that effect. Zehmer took a restaurant check and wrote on the back of it, "I do hereby agree to sell to W. O. Lucy the Ferguson Farm for $50,000 complete." Lucy told him he had better change it to "We" because Mrs. Zehmer would have to sign it too. Zehmer then tore up what he had written, wrote the agreement quoted above and asked Mrs. Zehmer, who was at the other end of the counter ten or twelve feet away, to sign it. Mrs. Zehmer said she would for $50,000 and signed it. Zehmer brought it back and gave it to Lucy, who offered him $5 which Zehmer refused, saying, "You don't need to give me any money, you got the agreement there signed by both of us."

The discussion leading to the signing of the agreement, said Lucy, lasted thirty or forty minutes, during which Zehmer seemed to doubt that Lucy could raise $50,000. Lucy suggested the provision for having the title examined and Zehmer made the suggestion that he would sell it "complete, everything there," and stated that all he had on the farm was three heifers.

Lucy took a partly filled bottle of whiskey into the restaurant with him for the purpose of giving Zehmer a drink if he wanted it. Zehmer did, and he and Lucy had one or two drinks together. Lucy said that while he felt the drinks he took he was not intoxicated, and from the way Zehmer handled the transaction he did not think he was either.

December 20 was on Saturday. Next day Lucy telephoned to J. C. Lucy and arranged with the latter to take a half interest in the purchase and pay half of the consideration. On Monday he engaged an attorney to examine the title. The attorney reported favorably on December 31 and on January 2 Lucy wrote Zehmer stating that the title was satisfactory, that he was ready to pay the purchase price in cash and asking when Zehmer would be ready to close the deal. Zehmer replied by letter, mailed on January 13, asserting that he had never agreed or intended to sell.

Mr. and Mrs. Zehmer were called by the complainants as adverse witnesses. Zehmer testified in substance as follows:

He bought this farm more than ten years ago for $11,000. He had had twenty-five offers, more or less, to buy it, including several from Lucy, who had never offered any specific sum of money. He had given them all the same answer, that he was not interested in selling it. On this Saturday night before Christmas it looked like everybody and his brother came by there to have a drink. He took a good many drinks during the afternoon and had a pint of his own. When he entered the restaurant around eight-thirty Lucy was there and he could see that he was "pretty high." He said to Lucy, "Boy, you got some good liquor, drinking, ain't you?" Lucy then offered him a drink. "I was already high as a Georgia pine, and didn't have any more better sense than to pour another great big slug out and gulp it down, and he took one too."

After they had talked a while Lucy asked whether he still had the Ferguson farm. He replied that he had not sold it and Lucy said, "I bet you wouldn't take $50,000 for it." Zehmer asked him if he would give $50,000 and Lucy said yes. Zehmer replied, "You haven't got $50,000 in cash." Lucy said he did and Zehmer replied that he did not believe it. They argued "pro and con for a long time," mainly about "whether he had $50,000 in cash that he could put up right then and buy that farm."

Finally, said Zehmer, Lucy told him if he didn't believe he had $50,000, "you sign that piece of paper here and say you will take $50,000.00 for the farm." He, Zehmer, "just grabbed the back off of a guest check there" and wrote on the back of it. At that point in his testimony Zehmer asked to see what he had written to "see if I recognize my own handwriting." He examined the paper and exclaimed, "Great balls of fire, I got 'Firgerson' for Ferguson. I have got satisfactory spelled wrong. I don't recognize that writing if I would see it, wouldn't know it was mine."

After Zehmer had, as he described it, "scribbled this thing off," Lucy said, "Get your wife to sign it." Zehmer walked over to where she was and she at first refused to sign but did so after he told her that he "was just needling him [Lucy], and didn't mean a thing in the world, that I was not selling the farm." Zehmer then "took it back over there and I was still looking at the dern thing. I had the drink right there by my hand, and I reached over to get a drink, and he said, 'Let me see it.' He reached and picked it up, and when I looked back again he had it in his pocket and he dropped a five dollar bill over there, and he said, 'Here is five dollars payment on it.' I said, 'Hell no, that is beer and liquor talking. I am not going to sell you the farm. I have told you that too many times before.'"

Mrs. Zehmer testified that when Lucy came into the restaurant he looked as if he had had a drink. When Zehmer came in he took a drink out of a bottle that Lucy handed him. She went back to help the waitress who was getting things ready for next day. Lucy and Zehmer were talking but she did not pay too much attention to what they were saying. She heard Lucy ask Zehmer if he had sold the Ferguson farm, and Zehmer replied that he had not and did not want to sell it. Lucy said, "I bet you wouldn't take $50,000 cash for that farm," and Zehmer replied, "You haven't got $50,000 cash." Lucy said, "I can get it." Zehmer said he might form a company and get it, "but you haven't got $50,000.00 cash to pay me tonight." Lucy asked him if he would put it in writing that he would sell him this farm. Zehmer then wrote on the back of a pad, "I agree to sell the Ferguson Place to W. O. Lucy for $50,000.00 cash." Lucy said, "All right, get your wife to sign it." Zehmer came back to where she was standing and said, "You want to put your name to this?" She said "No," but he said in an undertone, "It is nothing but a joke," and she signed it.

She said that only one paper was written and it said: "I hereby agree to sell," but the "I" had been changed to "We". However, she said she read what she signed and was then asked, "When you read 'We hereby agree to sell to W. O. Lucy,' what did you interpret that to mean, that particular phrase?" She said she thought that was a cash sale that night; but she also said that when she read that part about "title satisfactory to buyer" she understood that if the title was good Lucy would pay $50,000 but if the title was bad he would have a right to reject it, and that that was her understanding at the time she signed her name.

On examination by her own counsel she said that her husband laid this piece of paper down after it was signed; that Lucy said to let him see it, took it, folded it and put it in his wallet, then said to Zehmer, "Let me give you $5.00," but Zehmer said, "No, this is liquor talking. I don't want to sell the farm, I have told you that I want my son to have it. This is all a joke." Lucy then said at least twice, "Zehmer, you have sold your farm," wheeled around and started for the door. He paused at the door and said, "I will bring you $50,000.00 tomorrow. No, tomorrow is Sunday. I will bring it to you Monday." She said you could tell definitely that he was drinking and she said to her husband, "You should have taken him home," but he said, "Well, I am just about as bad off as he is."

The waitress referred to by Mrs. Zehmer testified that when Lucy first came in "he was mouthy." When Zehmer came in they were laughing and joking and she thought they took a drink or two. She was sweeping and cleaning up for next day. She said she heard Lucy tell Zehmer, "I will give you so much for the farm," and Zehmer said, "You haven't got that much." Lucy answered, "Oh, yes, I will give you that much." Then "they jotted down something on paper and Mr. Lucy reached over and took it, said let me see it." He looked at it, put it in his pocket and in about a minute he left. She was asked whether she saw Lucy offer Zehmer any money and replied, "He had five dollars laying up there, they didn't take it." She said Zehmer told Lucy he didn't want his money "because he didn't have enough money to pay for his property, and wasn't going to sell his farm." Both of them appeared to be drinking right much, she said.

She repeated on cross-examination that she was busy and paying no attention to what was going on. She was some distance away and did not see either of them sign the paper. She was asked whether she saw Zehmer put the agreement down on the table in front of Lucy, and her answer was this: "Time he got through writing whatever it was on the paper, Mr. Lucy reached over and said, 'Let's see it.' He took it and put it in his pocket," before showing it to Mrs. Zehmer. Her version was that Lucy kept raising his offer until it got to $50,000.

The defendants insist that the evidence was ample to support their contention that the writing sought to be enforced was prepared as a bluff or dare to force Lucy to admit that he did not have $50,000; that the whole matter was a joke; that the writing was not delivered to Lucy and no binding contract was ever made between the parties.

It is an unusual, if not bizarre, defense. When made to the writing admittedly prepared by one of the defendants and signed by both, clear evidence is required to sustain it.

In his testimony Zehmer claimed that he "was high as a Georgia pine," and that the transaction "was just a bunch of two doggoned drunks bluffing to see who could talk the biggest and say the most." That claim is inconsistent with his attempt to testify in great detail as to what was said and what was done. It is contradicted by other evidence as to the condition of both parties, and rendered of no weight by the testimony of his wife that when Lucy left the restaurant she suggested that Zehmer drive him home. The record is convincing that Zehmer was not intoxicated to the extent of being unable to comprehend the nature and consequences of the instrument he executed, and hence that instrument is not to be invalidated on that ground. 17 C.J.S., Contracts, § 133 b., p. 483; *Taliaferro v. Emery,* 124 Va. 674, 98 S.E. 627. It was in fact conceded by defendants' counsel in oral argument that under the evidence Zehmer was not too drunk to make a valid contract.

The evidence is convincing also that Zehmer wrote two agreements, the first one beginning "I hereby agree to sell." Zehmer first said he could not remember about that, then that "I don't think I wrote but one out." Mrs. Zehmer said that what he wrote was "I hereby agree," but that the "I" was changed to "We" after that night. The agreement that was written and signed is in the record and indicates no such change. Neither are the mistakes in spelling that Zehmer sought to point out readily apparent.

The appearance of the contract, the fact that it was under discussion for forty minutes or more before it was signed; Lucy's objection to the first draft because it was written in the singular, and he wanted Mrs. Zehmer to sign it also; the rewriting to meet that objection and the signing by Mrs. Zehmer; the discussion of what was to be included in the sale, the provision for the examination of the title, the completeness of the instrument that was executed, the taking possession of it by Lucy with no request or suggestion by either of the defendants that he give it back, are facts which furnish persuasive evidence that the execution of the contract was a serious business transaction rather than a casual, jesting matter as defendants now contend.

On Sunday, the day after the instrument was signed on Saturday night, there was a social gathering in a home in the town of McKenney at which there were general comments that the sale had been made. Mrs. Zehmer testified that on that occasion as she passed by a group of people, including Lucy, who were talking about the transaction, $50,000 was mentioned, where-upon she stepped up and said, "Well, with the high-price whiskey you were drinking last night you should have paid more. That was cheap." Lucy testified that at that time Zehmer told him that he did not want to "stick" him or hold him to the agreement because he, Lucy, was too tight and didn't know what he was doing, to which Lucy replied that he was not too tight; that he had been stuck before and was going through with it. Zehmer's version was that he said to Lucy: "I am not trying to claim it wasn't a deal on account of the fact the price was too low. If I had wanted to sell $50,000.00 would be a good price, in fact I think you would get stuck at $50,000.00." A disinterested witness testified that what Zehmer said to Lucy was that "he was going to let him up off the deal, because he thought he was too tight, didn't know what he was doing. Lucy said something to the effect that 'I have been stuck before and I will go through with it.'"

If it be assumed, contrary to what we think the evidence shows, that Zehmer was jesting about selling his farm to Lucy and that the transaction was intended by him to be a joke, nevertheless the evidence shows that Lucy did not so un-derstand it but considered it to be a serious business transaction and the contract to be binding on the Zehmers as well as on himself. The very next day he arranged with his brother to put up half the money and take a half interest in the land. The day after that he employed an attorney to examine the title. The next night, Tuesday, he was back at Zehmer's place and there Zehmer told him for the first time, Lucy said, that he wasn't going to sell and he told Zehmer, "You know you sold that place fair and square." After receiving the report from his attorney that the title was good he wrote to Zehmer that he was ready to close the deal.

Not only did Lucy actually believe, but the evidence shows he was warranted in believing, that the contract represented a serious business transaction and a good faith sale and purchase of the farm.

In the field of contracts, as generally elsewhere, "We must look to the outward expression of a person as manifesting his intention rather than to his secret and unexpressed intention. 'The law imputes to a person an intention corresponding to the reasonable meaning of his words and acts.'" *First Nat. Bank v. Roanoke Oil Co.,* 169 Va. 99, 114, 192 S.E. 764, 770.

At no time prior to the execution of the contract had Zehmer indicated to Lucy by word or act that he was not in earnest about selling the farm. They had argued about it and discussed its terms, as Zehmer admitted, for a long time. Lucy testified that if there was any jesting it was about paying $50,000 that night. The contract and the evidence show that he was not expected to pay the money that night. Zehmer said that after the writing was signed he laid it down on the counter in front of Lucy. Lucy said Zehmer handed it to him. In any event there had been what appeared to be a good faith offer and a good faith acceptance, followed by the execution and apparent delivery of a written contract. Both said that Lucy put the writing in his pocket and then offered Zehmer $5 to seal the bargain. Not until then, even under the defendants' evidence, was anything said or done to indicate that the matter was a joke. Both of the Zehmers testified that when Zehmer asked his wife to sign he whispered that it was a joke so Lucy wouldn't hear and that it was not intended that he should hear.

The mental assent of the parties is not requisite for the formation of a contract. If the words or other acts of one of the parties have but one reasonable meaning, his undisclosed intention is immaterial except when an unreasonable meaning which he attaches to his manifestations is known to the other party. Restatement of the Law of Contracts, Vol. I, §71, p. 74.

"The law, therefore, judges of an agreement between two persons exclusively from those expressions of their intentions which are communicated between them." Clark on Contracts, 4 ed., §3, p. 4.

An agreement or mutual assent is of course essential to a valid contract but the law imputes to a person an intention corresponding to the reasonable meaning of his words and acts. If his words and acts, judged by a reasonable standard, manifest an intention to agree, it is immaterial what may be the real but unexpressed state of his mind. 17 C.J.S., Contracts, §32, p. 361; 12 Am. Jur., Contracts, §19, p. 515.

So a person cannot set up that he was merely jesting when his conduct and words would warrant a reasonable person in believing that he intended a real agreement, 17 C.J.S., Contracts, §47, p. 390; Clark on Contracts, 4 ed., §27, at p. 54.

Whether the writing signed by the defendants and now sought to be enforced by the complainants was the result of a serious offer by Lucy and a serious acceptance by the defendants, or was a serious offer by Lucy and an acceptance in secret jest by the defendants, in either event it constituted a binding contract of sale between the parties.

Defendants contend further, however, that even though a contract was made, equity should decline to enforce it under the circumstances. These circumstances have been set forth in detail above. They disclose some drinking by the two parties but not to an extent that they were unable to understand fully what they were doing. There was no fraud, no misrepresentation, no sharp practice and no dealing between unequal parties. The farm had been bought for $11,000 and was assessed for taxation at $6,300. The purchase price was $50,000. Zehmer admitted that it was a good price. There is in fact present in this case none of the grounds usually urged against specific performance.

Specific performance, it is true, is not a matter of absolute or arbitrary right, but is addressed to the reasonable and sound discretion of the court. *First Nat. Bank v. Roanoke Oil Co., supra,* 169 Va. at p. 116, 192 S.E. at p. 771. But it is likewise true that the discretion which may be exercised is not an arbitrary or capricious one, but one which is controlled by the established doctrines and settled principles of equity; and, generally, where a contract is in its nature and circumstances unobjectionable, it is as much a matter of course for courts of equity to decree a specific performance of it as it is for a court of law to give damages for a breach of it. *Bond v. Crawford,* 193 Va. 437, 444, 69 S.E.(2d) 470, 475.

The complainants are entitled to have specific performance of the contracts sued on. The decree appealed from is therefore reversed and the cause is remanded for the entry of a proper decree requiring the defendants to perform the contract in accordance with the prayer of the bill.

Reversed and remanded.

From Chapter Three:

Crown Case Reserved, Ireland.

REGINA

v.

FAULKNER.

13 Cox C. C. 550

1877

CASE reserved by LAWSON, J., at the Cork Summer Assizes, 1876. The prisoner was indicted for setting fire to the ship "1 Zemindar," on the high seas, on the 26th day of June, 1876. The indictment was as follows: "That Robert Faulkner, on the 26th day of June, 1876, on board a certain ship called the 'Zemindar,' the property of Sandback, Tenue, and Co., on a certain voyage on the high seas, then being on the high seas, feloniously, unlawfully, and maliciously, did set fire to the said ship 'with intent thereby to prejudice the said' (these words were struck out at the trial by the learned judge, and the following words Inserted, 'called the "Zemindar," the property of') Sandback, Tenne, and Co., and that the said Robert Faulkner, on the day and year aforesaid, on board a certain ship called the 'Zemindar,' being the property of Sandback, Parker, and other, on a certain voyage on the high seas, then being upon the high seas, feloniously, unlawfully, and maliciously, did set fire to the said ship, with intent thereby to prejudice the said Sandback, Parker, and other, the owners of certain goods and chattels then laden, and being on board said ship." It was proved that the "Zemindar" was on her voyage home with a cargo of rum, sugar, and cotton, worth £50,000. That the prisoner was a seaman on board, that he went into the forecastle hold, opened the sliding door in the bulkhead, and so got into the hold where the rum was stored; he had no business there, and no authority to go there, and went for the purpose of stealing some rum; that he bored a hole in the cask with a gimlet; that the rum ran out; that when trying to put a spile in the hole out of which the rum was running he had a lighted match in his hand; that the rum caught fire; that the prisoner himself was burned on the arms and neck; and that the ship caught fire and was completely destroyed. At the close of the case for the Crown, counsel for the prisoner asked for a direction of an acquittal on the ground that on the facts proved the indictment was not sustained, nor the allegation that the prisoner had unlawfully and maliciously set fire to the ship proved. The Crown contended that inasmuch as the prisoner was at the time engaged in the commission of a felony, the indictment was sustained, and the allegation of the intent was immaterial.

At the second hearing of the case, before the Court for Crown Cases Reserved, the learned judge made the addition of the following paragraph to the case stated by him for the court.

"It was conceded that the prisoner had no actual intention of burning the vessel, and I was not asked to leave any question to the jury as to the prisoner's knowing the probable consequences of his act, or as to his reckless conduct."

The learned judge told the jury that although the prisoner had no actual intention of burning the vessel, still if they found he was engaged in stealing the rum, and that the fire took place in the manner above stated, they ought to find him guilty. The jury found the prisoner guilty on both counts, and he was sentenced to seven years' penal servitude. The question for the court was whether the direction of the learned judge was right; if not, the conviction should be quashed.

Peter O'Brien, for the prisoner.

The *Attorney General* (May), with him *Green*, Q. C., for the Crown.

O'BRIEN, J. I am also of opinion that the conviction should be quashed, and I was of that opinion before the case for our consideration was amended by my brother Lawson. I had inferred from the original case that his direction to the jury was to the effect now expressly stated by amendment, and that, at the trial, the Crown's counsel conceded that the prisoner had no intention of burning the vessel, or of igniting the rum; and raised no questions as to prisoner's imagining or having any ground for supposing that the fire would be the result or consequence of his act in stealing the rum. With respect to *Reg. v. Pembliton*, 12 Cox C. C. 607, it appears to me there were much stronger grounds in that case for upholding the conviction than exist in the case before us. In that case the breaking of the window was the act of the prisoner. He threw the stone that broke it; he threw it with the unlawful intent of striking some one of the crowd about, and the breaking of the window was the direct and immediate result of his act. And yet the court unanimously quashed the conviction upon the ground that, although the prisoner threw the stone intending to strike some one or more persons, he did not intend to break the window. The courts above have intimated their opinion that if the jury, upon a question to that effect being left to them, had found that the prisoner, knowing the window was there, might have reasonably expected that the result of his act would be the breaking of the window, that then the conviction should be upheld. During the argument of this case the Crown counsel required us to assume that the jury found their verdict upon the ground that in their opinion the prisoner may have expected that the fire would be the consequence of his act in stealing the rum, but nevertheless did the act recklessly, not caring whether the fire took place or not. But at the trial there was not even a suggestion of any such ground, and we cannot assume that the jury formed an opinion which there was no evidence to sustain, and which would be altogether inconsistent with the circumstances under which the fire took place. The reasonable inference from the evidence is that the prisoner lighted the match for the purpose of putting the spile in the hole to stop the further running of the rum, and that while he was attempting to do so, the rum came in contact with the lighted match and took fire. The recent case of *Reg. v. Welch*, 13 Cox C. C. 121, has been also referred to, and has been relied on by the Crown counsel on the ground that, though the jury found that the prisoner did not, in fact, intend to kill, maim, or wound the mare that had died from the injury inflicted by the prisoner, the prisoner was, nevertheless, convicted on an indictment charging him with having unlawfully and maliciously killed, maimed, or wounded the mare, and such conviction was upheld by the court. But on referring to the circumstances of that case it will be seen that the decision in it does not in any way conflict with that in the previous case of *Reg. v. Pembliton*, and furnishes no ground for sustaining the present conviction. Mr. Justice Lindley, who tried that subsequent case, appears to have acted in accordance with the opinion expressed by the judges in *Reg. v. Pembliton*. Besides leaving to the jury the question of prisoner's intent, he also left them a second question, namely, whether the prisoner, when he did the act complained of, knew that what he was doing would or might kill, maim, or wound the mare, and nevertheless did the act recklessly, and not caring whether the mare was injured or not. The jury answered that second question in the affirmative. Their finding was clearly warranted by the evidence, and the conviction was properly affirmed. By those two questions a distinction was taken between the case of an act done by a party with the actual intent to cause the injury inflicted, and the case of an act done by a party knowing or believing that it would or might cause such injury, but reckless of the result whether it did or did not. In the case now before us there was no ground whatever for submitting to the jury any question as to the prisoner believing or supposing that the stealing of the rum would be attended with a result so accidental and so dangerous to himself. During the argument doubts were suggested as to the soundness of the decision in *Reg. v. Pembliton*; but in my opinion that case was rightly decided, and should be followed. Its authority was not questioned in *Reg. v. Welch*, in which the judges who constituted the court were different from those who had decided *Reg. v. Pembliton*, with the exception of Lord Coleridge, who delivered the judgments of the court on both occasions.

PALLES, C. B. I concur in the opinion of the majority of the court, and I do so for the reasons already stated by my brother Fitzgerald. I agree with my brother Keogh that from the facts proved the inference might have been legitimately drawn that the setting fire to the ship was malicious within the meaning of the 24 & 25 Vict. c. 97. I am of opinion that that inference was one of fact for the jury, and not a conclusion of law at which we can arrive upon the case before us. There is one fact from which, if found, that inference would, in my opinion, have arisen as matter of law, as that the setting fire to the ship was the probable result of the prisoner's act in having a lighted match in the place in question; and if that had been found I should have concurred in the conclusion at which Mr. Justice Keogh has arrived. In my judgment the law imputes to a person who willfully commits a criminal act an intention to do everything which is the probable consequence of the act constituting the corpus delicti which actually ensues. In my opinion this inference arises irrespective of the particular consequence which ensued being or not being foreseen by the criminal, and whether his conduct is reckless or the reverse. This much I have deemed it right to say to prevent misconception as the grounds upon which my opinion is based. I wish to add one word as to *Reg. v. Pembliton*, 12 Cox C. C. 607. In my opinion the learned judges who were parties to that decision never intended to decide, and did not decide, anything contrary to the views I have expressed. That they did not deem actual intention, as distinguished from implied intention, essential is shown by the subsequent case of *Reg. v. Welch*, in which an indictment under the 40th section of the same Act was upheld, although actual intention was negatived by the jury. The facts found in answer to the second question in that case cannot have been relied upon as evidence of actual intention. As evidence they would have been valueless in face of the finding negativing the fact which in this view they would have but tended to prove. Their value was to indicate a state of facts in which intention was imputed by an irrefutable inference of law. It was not germane to the actual decisions in *Reg. v. Pembliton* and *Reg. v. Welch* to determine whether the state of facts from which this inference of law arises is that suggested in the first case and acted upon by the second, or the circumstance of one act being the natural consequence of the other. Some of the learned judges, no doubt, during the arguments and in their judgments in the first case indicate a state of facts from which this inference would arise. They do not decide that the same inference might not arise in the other state of facts to which I have alluded. If, contrary to my own view of that case, it shall be held to involve that intention to do that which is a necessary consequence of a wrongful act willfully committed is not an inference irrefutable as matter of law, I must say, with unfeigned deference, that I shall hold myself free hereafter to decline to follow it. The Lord-Chief Justice of the Common Pleas, who, in consequence of illness, has been unable to preside to-day, has authorized me to state that he considers that the case before us is concluded by *Reg. v. Pembliton*.

Conviction quashed.

From Chapter Three:

144 Vt. 150

Supreme Court of Vermont.

Ella HILDER

v.

Stuart ST. PETER and Patricia St. Peter.

No. 82-440.

Feb. 3, 1984. Reargument Denied May 4, 1984.

BILLINGS, Chief Justice.

Defendants appeal from a judgment rendered by the Rutland Superior Court. The court ordered defendants to pay plaintiff damages in the amount of $4,945.00, which represented "reimbursement of all rent paid and additional compensatory damages" for the rental of a residential apartment over a fourteen month period in defendants' Rutland apartment building. Defendants filed a motion for reconsideration on the issue of the amount of damages awarded to the plaintiff, and plaintiff filed a cross-motion for reconsideration of the court's denial of an award of punitive damages. The court denied both motions. On appeal, defendants raise three issues for our consideration: first, whether the court correctly calculated the amount of damages awarded the plaintiff; secondly, whether the court's award to plaintiff of the entire amount of rent paid to defendants was proper since the plaintiff remained in possession of the apartment for the entire fourteen month period; and finally, whether the court's finding that defendant Stuart St. Peter acted on his own behalf and with the apparent authority of defendant Patricia St. Peter was error.

The facts are uncontested. In October, 1974, plaintiff began occupying an apartment at defendants' 10-12 Church Street apartment building in Rutland with her three children and new-born grandson. Plaintiff orally agreed to pay defendant Stuart St. Peter $140 a month and a damage deposit of $50; plaintiff paid defendant the first month's rent and the damage deposit prior to moving in. Plaintiff has paid all rent due under her tenancy. Because the previous tenants had left behind garbage and items of personal belongings, defendant offered to refund plaintiff's damage deposit if she would clean the apartment herself prior to taking possession. Plaintiff did clean the apartment, but never received her deposit back because the defendant denied ever receiving it. Upon moving into the apartment, plaintiff discovered a broken kitchen window. Defendant promised to repair it, but after waiting a week and fearing that her two year old child might cut herself on the shards of glass, plaintiff repaired the window at her own expense. Although defendant promised to provide a front door key, he never did. For a period of time, whenever plaintiff left the apartment, a member of her family would remain behind for security reasons. Eventually, plaintiff purchased and installed a padlock, again at her own expense. After moving in, plaintiff discovered that the bathroom toilet was clogged with paper and feces and would flush only by dumping pails of water into it. Although plaintiff repeatedly complained about the toilet, and defendant promised to have it repaired, the toilet remained clogged and mechanically inoperable throughout the period of plaintiff's tenancy. In addition, the bathroom light and wall outlet were inoperable. Again, the defendant agreed to repair the fixtures, but never did. In order to have light in the bathroom, plaintiff attached a fixture to the wall and connected it to an extension cord that was plugged into an adjoining room. Plaintiff also discovered that water leaked from the water pipes of the upstairs apartment down the ceilings and walls of both her kitchen and back bedroom. Again, defendant promised to fix the leakage, but never did. As a result of this leakage, a large section of plaster fell from the back bedroom ceiling onto her bed and her grandson's crib. Other sections of plaster remained dangling from the ceiling. This condition was brought to the attention of the defendant, but he never corrected it. Fearing that the remaining plaster might fall when the room was occupied, plaintiff moved her and her grandson's bedroom furniture into the living room and ceased using the back bedroom. During the summer months an odor of raw sewage permeated plaintiff's apartment. The odor was so strong that the plaintiff was ashamed to have company in her apartment. Responding to plaintiff's complaints, Rutland City workers unearthed a broken sewage pipe in the basement of defendants' building. Raw sewage littered the floor of the basement, but defendant failed to clean it up. Plaintiff also discovered that the electric service for her furnace was attached to her breaker box, although defendant had agreed, at the commencement of plaintiff's tenancy, to furnish heat.

In its conclusions of law, the court held that the state of disrepair of plaintiff's apartment, which was known to the defendants, substantially reduced the value of the leasehold from the agreed rental value, thus constituting a breach of the implied warranty of habitability. The court based its award of damages on the breach of this warranty and on breach of an express contract. Defendant argues that the court misapplied the law of Vermont relating to habitability because the plaintiff never abandoned the demised premises and, therefore, it was error to award her the full amount of rent paid. Plaintiff counters that, while never expressly recognized by this Court, the trial court was correct in applying an implied warranty of habitability and that under this warranty, abandonment of the premises is not required. Plaintiff urges this Court to affirmatively adopt the implied warranty of habitability.

Historically, relations between landlords and tenants have been defined by the law of property. Under these traditional common law property concepts, a lease was viewed as a conveyance of real property. See Note, *Judicial Expansion of Tenants' Private Law Rights: Implied Warranties of Habitability and Safety in Residential Urban Leases*, 56 Cornell L.Q. 489, 489–90 (1971) (hereinafter cited as *Expansion of Tenants' Rights*). The relationship between landlord and tenant was controlled by the doctrine of caveat lessee; that is, the tenant took possession of the demised premises irrespective of their state of disrepair. Love, *Landlord's Liability for Defective Premises: Caveat Lessee, Negligence, or Strict Liability?*, 1975 Wis.L. Rev. 19, 27–28. The landlord's only covenant was to deliver possession to the tenant. The tenant's obligation to pay rent existed independently of the landlord's duty to deliver possession, so that as long as possession remained in the tenant, the tenant remained liable for payment of rent. The landlord was under no duty to render the premises habitable unless there was an express covenant to repair in the written lease. *Expansion of Tenants' Rights, supra*, at 490. The land, not the dwelling, was regarded as the essence of the conveyance.

An exception to the rule of caveat lessee was the doctrine of constructive eviction. *Lemle v. Breeden*, 51 Haw. 426, 430, 462 P.2d 470, 473 (1969). Here, if the landlord wrongfully interfered with the tenant's enjoyment of the demised premises, or failed to render a duty to the tenant as expressly required under the terms of the lease, the tenant could abandon the premises and cease paying rent. *Legier v. Deveneau*, 98 Vt. 188, 190, 126 A. 392, 393 (1924).

Beginning in the 1960s, American courts began recognizing that this approach to landlord and tenant relations, which had originated during the Middle Ages, had become an anachronism in twentieth century, urban society. Today's tenant enters into lease agreements, not to obtain arable land, but to obtain safe, sanitary and comfortable housing.

> [T]hey seek a well known package of goods and services — a package which includes not merely walls and ceilings, but also adequate heat, light and ventilation, serviceable plumbing facilities, secure windows and doors, proper sanitation, and proper maintenance.

Javins v. First National Realty Corp., 428 F.2d 1071, 1074 (D.C.Cir.), *cert. denied*, 400 U.S. 925, 91 S.Ct. 186, 27 L.Ed.2d 185 (1970).

Not only has the subject matter of today's lease changed, but the characteristics of today's tenant have similarly evolved. The tenant of the Middle Ages was a farmer, capable of making whatever repairs were necessary to his primitive dwelling. *Green v. Superior Court,* 10 Cal.3d 616, 622, 517 P.2d 1168, 1172, 111 Cal.Rptr. 704, 708 (1974). Additionally, "the common law courts assumed that an equal bargaining position existed between landlord and tenant...." Note, *The Implied Warranty of Habitability: A Dream Deferred,* 48 UMKC L.Rev. 237, 238 (1980) (hereinafter cited as *A Dream Deferred*).

In sharp contrast, today's residential tenant, most commonly a city dweller, is not experienced in performing maintenance work on urban, complex living units. *Green v. Superior Court, supra,* 10 Cal.3d at 624, 517 P.2d at 1173, 111 Cal.Rptr. at 707–08. The landlord is more familiar with the dwelling unit and mechanical equipment attached to that unit, and is more financially able to "discover and cure" any faults and break-downs. *Id.* at 624, 517 P.2d at 1173, 111 Cal.Rptr. at 708. Confronted with a recognized shortage of safe, decent housing, see 24 V.S.A. §4001(1), today's tenant is in an inferior bargaining position compared to that of the landlord. *Park West Management Corp. v. Mitchell,* 47 N.Y.2d 316, 324–25, 391 N.E.2d 1288, 1292, 418 N.Y.S.2d 310, 314, *cert. denied,* 444 U.S. 992, 100 S.Ct. 523, 62 L.Ed.2d 421 (1979). Tenants vying for this limited housing are "virtually powerless to compel the performance of essential services." *Id.* at 325, 391 N.E.2d at 1292, 418 N.Y.S.2d at 314.

In light of these changes in the relationship between tenants and landlords, it would be wrong for the law to continue to impose the doctrine of caveat lessee on residential leases.

> The modern view favors a new approach which recognizes that a lease is essentially a contract between the landlord and the tenant wherein the landlord promises to deliver and maintain the demised premises in habitable condition and the tenant promises to pay rent for such habitable premises. These promises constitute interdependent and mutual considerations. Thus, the tenant's obligation to pay rent is predicated on the landlord's obligation to deliver and maintain the premises in habitable condition.

Boston Housing Authority v. Hemingway, 363 Mass. 184, 198, 293 N.E.2d 831, 842 (1973).

Recognition of residential leases as contracts embodying the mutual covenants of habitability and payment of rent does not represent an abrupt change in Vermont law. Our case law has previously recognized that contract remedies are available for breaches of lease agreements. *Clarendon Mobile Home Sales, Inc. v. Fitzgerald,* 135 Vt. 594, 596, 381 A.2d 1063, 1065 (1977); *Keene v. Willis,* 128 Vt. 187, 188, 191–92, 260 A.2d 371, 371–72, 374 (1969); *Breese v. McCann,* 52 Vt. 498, 501 (1879). More significantly, our legislature, in establishing local housing authorities, 24 V.S.A. §4003, has officially recognized the need for assuring the existence of adequate housing.

> [S]ubstandard and decadent areas exist in certain portions of the state of Vermont and ... there is not ... an adequate supply of decent, safe and sanitary housing for persons of low income and/or elderly persons of low income, available for rents which such persons can afford to pay ... this situation tends to cause an increase and spread of communicable and chronic disease ... [and] constitutes a menace to the health, safety, welfare and comfort of the inhabitants of the state and is detrimental to property values in the localities in which it exists....

24 V.S.A. §4001(4). In addition, this Court has assumed the existence of an implied warranty of habitability in residential leases. *Birkenhead v. Coombs*, 143 Vt. 167, 172, 465 A.2d 244, 246 (1983).

Therefore, we now hold expressly that in the rental of any residential dwelling unit an implied warranty exists in the lease, whether oral or written, that the landlord will deliver over and maintain, throughout the period of the tenancy, premises that are safe, clean and fit for human habitation. This warranty of habitability is implied in tenancies for a specific period or at will. *Boston Housing Authority v. Hemingway, supra*, 363 Mass. at 199, 293 N.E.2d at 843. Additionally, the implied warranty of habitability covers all latent and patent defects in the essential facilities of the residential unit. *Id.* Essential facilities are "facilities vital to the use of the premises for residential purposes...." *Kline v. Burns*, 111 N.H. 87, 92, 276 A.2d 248, 252 (1971). This means that a tenant who enters into a lease agreement with knowledge of any defect in the essential facilities cannot be said to have assumed the risk, thereby losing the protection of the warranty. Nor can this implied warranty of habitability be waived by any written provision in the lease or by oral agreement.

In determining whether there has been a breach of the implied warranty of habitability, the courts may first look to any relevant local or municipal housing code; they may also make reference to the minimum housing code standards enunciated in 24 V.S.A. §5003(c)(1)-5003(c)(5). A substantial violation of an applicable housing code shall constitute prima facie evidence that there has been a breach of the warranty of habitability. "[O]ne or two minor violations standing alone which do not affect" the health or safety of the tenant, shall be considered de minimus and not a breach of the warranty. *Javins v. First National Realty Corp., supra*, 428 F.2d at 1082 n. 63; *Mease v. Fox*, 200 N.W.2d 791, 796 (Iowa 1972); *King v. Moorehead, supra*, 495 S.W.2d at 76. In addition, the landlord will not be liable for defects caused by the tenant. *Javins v. First National Realty Corp., supra*, 428 F.2d at 1082 n. 62.

However, these codes and standards merely provide a starting point in determining whether there has been a breach. Not all towns and municipalities have housing codes; where there are codes, the particular problem complained of may not be addressed. *Park West Management Corp. v. Mitchell, supra,* 47 N.Y.2d at 328, 391 N.E.2d at 1294, 418 N.Y.S.2d at 316. In determining whether there has been a breach of the implied warranty of habitability, courts should inquire whether the claimed defect has an impact on the safety or health of the tenant. *Id.*

In order to bring a cause of action for breach of the implied warranty of habitability, the tenant must first show that he or she notified the landlord "of the deficiency or defect not known to the landlord and [allowed] a reasonable time for its correction." *King v. Moorehead, supra,* 495 S.W.2d at 76.

Because we hold that the lease of a residential dwelling creates a contractual relationship between the landlord and tenant, the standard contract remedies of rescission, reformation and damages are available to the tenant when suing for breach of the implied warranty of habitability. *Lemle v. Breeden, supra,* 51 Haw. at 436, 462 P.2d at 475. The measure of damages shall be the difference between the value of the dwelling as warranted and the value of the dwelling as it exists in its defective condition. *Birkenhead v. Coombs, supra,* 143 Vt. at 172, 465 A.2d at 246. In determining the fair rental value of the dwelling as warranted, the court may look to the agreed upon rent as evidence on this issue. *Id.* "[I]n residential lease disputes involving a breach of the implied warranty of habitability, public policy militates against requiring expert testimony" concerning the value of the defect. *Id.* at 173, 465 A.2d at 247. The tenant will be liable only for "the reasonable rental value [if any] of the property in its imperfect condition during his period of occupancy." *Berzito v. Gambino,* 63 N.J. 460, 469, 308 A.2d 17, 22 (1973).

We also find persuasive the reasoning of some commentators that damages should be allowed for a tenant's discomfort and annoyance arising from the landlord's breach of the implied warranty of habitability. See Moskovitz, *The Implied Warranty of Habitability: A New Doctrine Raising New Issues,* 62 Calif.L. Rev. 1444, 1470–73 (1974) (hereinafter cited as *A New Doctrine*); *A Dream Deferred, supra,* at 250–51. Damages for annoyance and discomfort are reasonable in light of the fact that

> the residential tenant who has suffered a breach of the warranty ... cannot bathe as frequently as he would like or at all if there is inadequate hot water; he must worry about rodents harassing his children or spreading disease if the premises are infested; or he must avoid certain rooms or worry about catching a cold if there is inadequate weather protection or heat. Thus, discomfort and annoyance are the common injuries caused

by each breach and hence the true nature of the general damages the tenant is claiming.

Moskovitz, *A New Doctrine, supra,* at 1470–71. Damages for discomfort and annoyance may be difficult to compute; however, "[t]he trier [of fact] is not to be deterred from this duty by the fact that the damages are not susceptible of reduction to an exact money standard." *Vermont Electric Supply Co. v. Andrus,* 132 Vt. 195, 200, 315 A.2d 456, 459 (1974).

Another remedy available to the tenant when there has been a breach of the implied warranty of habitability is to withhold the payment of future rent. *King v. Moorehead, supra,* 495 S.W.2d at 77. The burden and expense of bringing suit will then be on the landlord who can better afford to bring the action. In an action for ejectment for nonpayment of rent, 12 V.S.A. § 4773, "[t]he trier of fact, upon evaluating the seriousness of the breach and the ramification of the defect upon the health and safety of the tenant, will abate the rent at the landlord's expense in accordance with its findings." *A Dream Deferred, supra,* at 248. The tenant must show that: (1) the landlord had notice of the previously unknown defect and failed, within a reasonable time, to repair it; and (2) the defect, affecting habitability, existed during the time for which rent was withheld. See *A Dream Deferred, supra,* at 248–50. Whether a portion, all or none of the rent will be awarded to the landlord will depend on the findings relative to the extent and duration of the breach. *Javins v. First National Realty Corp., supra,* 428 F.2d at 1082–83. Of course, once the landlord corrects the defect, the tenant's obligation to pay rent becomes due again. *Id.* at 1083 n. 64.

Additionally, we hold that when the landlord is notified of the defect but fails to repair it within a reasonable amount of time, and the tenant subsequently repairs the defect, the tenant may deduct the expense of the repair from future rent. 11 Williston on Contracts § 1404 (3d ed. W. Jaeger 1968); *Marini v. Ireland,* 56 N.J. 130, 146, 265 A.2d 526, 535 (1970).

In addition to general damages, we hold that punitive damages may be available to a tenant in the appropriate case. Although punitive damages are generally not recoverable in actions for breach of contract, there are cases in which the breach is of such a willful and wanton or fraudulent nature as to make appropriate the award of exemplary damages. *Clarendon Mobile Home Sales, Inc. v. Fitzgerald, supra,* 135 Vt. at 596, 381 A.2d at 1065. A willful and wanton or fraudulent breach may be shown "by conduct manifesting personal ill will, or carried out under circumstances of insult or oppression, or even by conduct manifesting ... a reckless or wanton disregard of [one's] rights...." *Sparrow v. Vermont Savings Bank,* 95 Vt. 29, 33, 112 A. 205, 207 (1921). When a landlord, after receiving notice of a defect, fails to repair the facility that is essential to the health and safety of his or her tenant, an award of punitive damages is proper. *111 East 88th Partners v. Simon,* 106 Misc.2d 693, 434 N.Y.S.2d 886, 889 (N.Y.Civ.Ct.1980).

> The purpose of punitive damages ... is to punish conduct which is morally culpable.... Such an award serves to deter a wrongdoer ... from repetitions of the same or similar actions. And it tends to encourage prosecution of a claim by a victim who might not otherwise incur the expense or inconvenience of private action.... The public benefit and a display of ethical indignation are among the ends of the policy to grant punitive damages.

Davis v. Williams, 92 Misc.2d 1051, 402 N.Y.S.2d 92, 94 (N.Y.Civ.Ct.1977).

In the instant case, the trial court's award of damages, based in part on a breach of the implied warranty of habitability, was not a misapplication of the law relative to habitability. Because of our holding in this case, the doctrine of constructive eviction, wherein the tenant must abandon in order to escape liability for rent, is no longer viable. When, as in the instant case, the tenant seeks, not to escape rent liability, but to receive compensatory damages in the amount of rent already paid, abandonment is similarly unnecessary. *Northern Terminals, Inc. v. Smith Grocery & Variety, Inc., supra,* 138 Vt. at 396–97, 418 A.2d at 26–27. Under our holding, when a landlord breaches the implied warranty of habitability, the tenant may withhold future rent, and may also seek damages in the amount of rent previously paid.

In its conclusions of law the trial court stated that the defendants' failure to make repairs was compensable by damages to the extent of reimbursement of all rent paid and additional compensatory damages. The court awarded plaintiff a total of $4,945.00; $3,445.00 represents the entire amount of rent plaintiff paid, plus the $50.00 deposit. This appears to leave $1500.00 as the "additional compensatory damages." However, although the court made findings which clearly demonstrate the appropriateness of an award of compensatory damages, there is no indication as to how the court reached a figure of $1500.00. It is "crucial that this Court and the parties be able to determine what was decided and how the decision was reached." *Fox v. McLain,* 142 Vt. 11, 16, 451 A.2d 1122, 1124 (1982).

Additionally, the court denied an award to plaintiff of punitive damages on the ground that the evidence failed to support a finding of willful and wanton or fraudulent conduct. See *Clarendon Mobile Home Sales, Inc. v. Fitzgerald, supra,* 135 Vt. at 596, 381 A.2d at 1065. The facts in this case, which defendants do not contest, evince a pattern of intentional conduct on the part of defendants for which the term "slumlord" surely was coined. Defendants' conduct was culpable and demeaning to plaintiff and clearly expressive of a wanton disregard of plaintiff's rights. The trial court found that defendants were aware of defects in the essential facilities of plaintiff's apartment, promised plaintiff that repairs would be made, but never fulfilled those promises. The court also found that plaintiff continued, throughout her tenancy, to pay her rent, often in the face of verbal threats made by defendant Stuart St. Peter. These findings point to the "bad spirit and wrong intention" of the defendants, *Glidden v. Skinner,* 142 Vt. 644, 648, 458 A.2d 1142, 1144 (1983), and would support a finding of willful and wanton or fraudulent conduct, contrary to the conclusions of law and judgment of the trial judge. However, the plaintiff did not appeal the court's denial of punitive damages, and issues not appealed and briefed are waived. *R. Brown & Sons, Inc. v. International Harvester Corp.,* 142 Vt. 140, 142, 453 A.2d 83, 84 (1982).

We find that defendants' third claimed error, that the court erred in finding that both defendant Stuart St. Peter and defendant Patricia St. Peter were liable to plaintiff for the breach of the implied warranty of habitability, is meritless. Both defendants were named in the complaint as owners of the 10-12 Church Street apartment building. Plaintiff's complaint also alleged that defendant Stuart St. Peter acted as agent for defendant Patricia St. Peter. Defendants failed to deny these allegations; under V.R.C.P. 8(d) these averments stand as admitted.

Affirmed in part; reversed in part and remanded for hearing on additional compensable damages, consistent with the views herein.

From Chapter Six:

Selected Federal Rules of Evidence
Effective July 1, 1975, Including Amendments Effective December 1, 2011

Rule 401. Test for Relevant Evidence

Evidence is relevant if:

(a) it has any tendency to make a fact more or less probable than it would be without the evidence;

and

(b) the fact is of consequence in determining the action.

Rule 403. Excluding Relevant Evidence for Prejudice, Confusion, Waste of Time, or Other Reasons

The court may exclude relevant evidence if its probative value is substantially outweighed by a danger of one or more of the following: unfair prejudice, confusing the issues, misleading the jury, undue delay, wasting time, or needlessly presenting cumulative evidence.

Rule 404. Character Evidence; Crimes or Other Acts

(a) Character Evidence.

(1) Prohibited Uses. Evidence of a person's character or character trait is not admissible to prove that on a particular occasion the person acted in accordance with the character or trait.

(2) Exceptions for a Defendant or Victim in a Criminal Case. The following exceptions apply in a criminal case:

(A) a defendant may offer evidence of the defendant's pertinent trait, and if the evidence is admitted, the prosecutor may offer evidence to rebut it;

(B) subject to the limitations in Rule 412, a defendant may offer evidence of an alleged victim's pertinent trait, and if the evidence is admitted, the prosecutor may:

(i) offer evidence to rebut it; and

(ii) offer evidence of the defendant's same trait; and

(C) in a homicide case, the prosecutor may offer evidence of the alleged victim's trait of peacefulness to rebut evidence that the victim was the first aggressor.

(3) Exceptions for a Witness. Evidence of a witness's character may be admitted under Rules 607, 608, and 609.

(b) Crimes, Wrongs, or Other Acts.

(1) Prohibited Uses. Evidence of a crime, wrong, or other act is not admissible to prove a person's character in order to show that on a particular occasion the person acted in accordance with the character.

(2) Permitted Uses; Notice in a Criminal Case. This evidence may be admissible for another purpose, such as proving motive, opportunity, intent, preparation, plan, knowledge, identity, absence of mistake, or lack of accident. On request by a defendant in a criminal case, the prosecutor must·

(A) provide reasonable notice of the general nature of any such evidence that the prosecutor intends to offer at trial; and

(B) do so before trial—or during trial if the court, for good cause, excuses lack of pretrial notice.

Rule 405. Methods of Proving Character

(a) By Reputation or Opinion. When evidence of a person's character or character trait is admissible, it may be proved by testimony about the person's reputation or by testimony in the form of an opinion. On cross-examination of the character witness, the court may allow an inquiry into relevant specific instances of the person's conduct.

(b) By Specific Instances of Conduct. When a person's character or character trait is an essential element of a charge, claim, or defense, the character or trait may also be proved by relevant specific instances of the person's conduct.

Rule 602. Need for Personal Knowledge

A witness may not testify to a matter unless evidence is introduced sufficient to support a finding that the witness has personal knowledge of the matter. Evidence to prove personal knowledge may, but need not, consist of the witness's own testimony. This rule does not apply to a witness's expert testimony under Rule 703.

Rule 608. A Witness's Character for Truthfulness or Untruthfulness

(a) Reputation or Opinion Evidence. A witness's credibility may be attacked or supported by testimony about the witness's reputation for having a character for truthfulness or untruthfulness, or by testimony in the form of an opinion about that character. But evidence of truthful character is admissible only after the witness's character for truthfulness has been attacked.

(b) Specific Instances of Conduct. Except for a criminal conviction under Rule 609, extrinsic evidence is not admissible to prove specific instances of a witness's conduct in order to attack or support the witness's character for truthfulness. But the court may, on cross-examination, allow them to be inquired into if they are probative of the character for truthfulness or untruthfulness of:

(1) the witness; or

(2) another witness whose character the witness being cross-examined has testified about.

By testifying on another matter, a witness does not waive any privilege against self-incrimination for testimony that relates only to the witness's character for truthfulness.

Rule 701. Opinion Testimony by Lay Witnesses

If a witness is not testifying as an expert, testimony in the form of an opinion is limited to one that is:

(a) rationally based on the witness's perception;

(b) helpful to clearly understanding the witness's testimony or to determining a fact in issue; and

(c) not based on scientific, technical, or other specialized knowledge within the scope of Rule 702.

Rule 702. Testimony by Expert Witnesses

A witness who is qualified as an expert by knowledge, skill, experience, training, or education may testify in the form of an opinion or otherwise if:

(a) the expert's scientific, technical, or other specialized knowledge will help the trier of fact to understand the evidence or to determine a fact in issue;

(b) the testimony is based on sufficient facts or data;

(c) the testimony is the product of reliable principles and methods; and

(d) the expert has reliably applied the principles and methods to the facts of the case.

Rule 801. Definitions That Apply to This Article; Exclusions from Hearsay

(a) Statement. "Statement" means a person's oral assertion, written assertion, or nonverbal conduct, if the person intended it as an assertion.

(b) Declarant. "Declarant" means the person who made the statement.

(c) Hearsay. "Hearsay" means a statement that:

(1) the declarant does not make while testifying at the current trial or hearing; and

(2) a party offers in evidence to prove the truth of the matter asserted in the statement.

(d) Statements That Are Not Hearsay. A statement that meets the following conditions is not hearsay:

(1) A Declarant-Witness's Prior Statement. The declarant testifies and is subject to cross-examination about a prior statement, and the statement:

(A) is inconsistent with the declarant's testimony and was given under penalty of perjury at a trial, hearing, or other proceeding or in a deposition;

(B) is consistent with the declarant's testimony and is offered to rebut an express or implied charge that the declarant recently fabricated it or acted from a recent improper influence or motive in so testifying; or

(C) identifies a person as someone the declarant perceived earlier.

(2) An Opposing Party's Statement. The statement is offered against an opposing party and:

(A) was made by the party in an individual or representative capacity;

(B) is one the party manifested that it adopted or believed to be true;

(C) was made by a person whom the party authorized to make a statement on the subject;

(D) was made by the party's agent or employee on a matter within the scope of that relationship and while it existed; or

(E) was made by the party's co-conspirator during and in furtherance of the conspiracy.

The statement must be considered but does not by itself establish the declarant's authority under (C); the existence or scope of the relationship under (D); or the existence of the conspiracy or participation in it under (E).

Rule 803. Exceptions to the Rule Against Hearsay—Regardless of Whether the Declarant Is Available as a Witness

The following are not excluded by the rule against hearsay, regardless of whether the declarant is available as a witness:

...

(8) *Public Records*. A record or statement of a public office if:

(A) it sets out:

(i) the office's activities;

(ii) a matter observed while under a legal duty to report, but not including, in a criminal case, a matter observed by law-enforcement personnel; or

(iii) in a civil case or against the government in a criminal case, factual findings from a legally authorized investigation; and

(B) neither the source of information nor other circumstances indicate a lack of trustworthiness.

Index

1

1L year. *See* First year of law school

A

Actor's neutral. *See* Gestures

Affidavit, 100

Alito, Samuel, 78

Analogies, use of. *See* Legal reasoning

Anecdotes, use of

In presentations, 56

Appellate advocacy. *See* Moot court

Aristotle, 22–24, 52–53, 119, 151

Attorney-client privilege, 143

Authentication of evidence

During trial, 96–97

Availability heuristic, 24

B

Barnhart v. Peabody Coal Co., 73

Becoming Gentlemen, 33

Binding vs. persuasive authority, 20, 21–22, 77

Body movement/language

During trial, 92–93

When making presentations, 55, 58, 60–62

Brandeis, Louis, 19

Briefs

Case briefs. *See* Case-briefing

Legal briefs, 25, 72, 76

Burden of proof/persuasion, 43, 85, 86

C

Callback interviews. *See* Interviewing for a job

Career services office, working with, 129, 133

Carlson, Tucker, 139–140

Case-briefing, 25–29

Cases. *See* Reading for class

Chambers and Partners, 130

Citizens United v. Federal Election Commission, 78

Civil law, 18

Class discussions, 17, 32, 51, 117–119

Classroom distractions, 31–32, 118

Closing arguments. *See* Trial

Cold calls. *See* Socratic Method

Common law, 18, 24, 101

Common Socratic questions, 43–45

Communicating on the job. *See* Workplace communication
Confidence, importance of projecting
 During job interviews, 126, 131–133, 134
 During trial, 87, 88, 99
 Socratic Method, and, 8, 33, 36, 41–43, 49
 When making presentations, 54, 58, 59, 60, 61, 62, 65, 68, 69
Conservatism, legal, 19
Contract law, 3–8, 25–29, 87, 88
Course evaluations, 32, 59, 120
Course outlines. *See* Outlining
Courses in law school
 Evidence, 101
 Legal research and writing, 71–81
 Oral advocacy/public speaking classes, 34, 43, 137
 Trial practice, 83–106
Criminal law, 37–41
Cross-examination. *See* Trial

D

Deductive reasoning. *See* Legal reasoning
Dicta. *See* Holding/dicta distinction
Direct examination. *See* Trial
District of Columbia v. Heller, 21

E

E-mail, use of
 In a student organization, 114
 On the job, 142–143
 When interacting with professors, 119–120
Ethos, 36, 52–53, 54, 57, 58, 59, 63, 64, 86–88, 90, 106, 119, 132, 151

Exams. *See* Final exams
Exhibits
 Entering into evidence during trial, 89, 95, 96–97
Extracurricular activities. *See* Student organizations
Eye contact
 During job interviews, 133, 136
 During trial, 93, 94
 In the classroom, 36
 On the job, 147
 When making presentations, 58, 61, 63, 65–66

F

Federal Rules of Evidence, 95, 97, 101–105, 180–184
Filler sounds, use of, 5, 33, 36, 64, 131, 132
Final exams
 Outlining, and, 29–30
 Socratic Method, and, 9, 14, 17
 Study habits, and, 16–17
First Amendment, 78, 79–80
First year of law school
 Legal research and writing courses, 71–81
 Reading for class, and, 34
 Socratic Method, and, 24, 33, 36, 41

G

Gestures, use of
 When making presentations, 62–63
Grades
 Job interviews, and, 10, 128–130, 139
 Socratic Method, and, *x*, 9, 14, 17

Working as a lawyer, and, 10
Guinier, Lani, 33
Gunners, 32

H
Harvard Law School, 8
Hearsay, 97, 102, 104–105, 182–184
Highlighting. *See* Reading for class
Hilder v. St. Peter, 45–48, 171–179
Holding/dicta distinction, 20
Hypotheticals, use of
    In moot court, 73, 78
    Socratic Method, and, 6–7, 20,
      22, 34, 44

I
I Have a Dream speech, 66
Impeaching a witness. *See* Trial
Inductive reasoning. *See* Legal rea-
    soning
Interviewing for a job, 125–140
    Callback interviews, 126, 130,
      134, 137–139
    Grades, and, 139
    On-campus interviews, 125–126
    Practicing for an interview, 126,
      131–133, 134–135, 137
      Nonverbal communication,
        132–133
      Vocal tips, 131–132
    Preparing for an interview, 126–
      131
      Basic interview questions,
        130–131
      Dealing with bad facts, 128–
        130
      Know why you want the job,
        127–128
      Knowing current events, 130
      Knowing the employer, 130

Knowing your classes, 130
Knowing your resume, 126–
    127
Theme, and use of, 126, 127,
    128, 136, 137
Tone, and use of, 131, 137
What to do during the interview,
    136–137
What to wear/bring to the inter-
    view, 133–135

J
Jargon, use of, x, 56, 57, 59, 79, 88
Job communications/interactions.
    See Workplace communication
Job interviews. *See* Interviewing for
    a job

K
Kagan, Elena, 78
Kiernan, Peter, 142
King, Martin Luther, 66

L
Langdell, Christopher Columbus, 8
Laptops, use of
    In class. *See* Classroom distrac-
      tions
    To e-mail. *See* E-mail, use of
Law firms
    Communicating with others in,
      9–10, 141–149
    Getting assignments while work-
      ing for, x, 9–10
    Interviewing for, 125–140
    Making presentations in, 51–52,
      68
    Social events at, 147–149
    Summer associate work in, 10,
      51–52, 141–149

Leading questions, use of
   During trial, 94, 99
Legal reasoning
   Analogies, use of, 22
   Avoiding logical fallacies, 22–24
   Deductive reasoning, use of, 22–
      23
   Inductive reasoning, use of, 23–
      24
   Precedent, use of, 19–20, 21, 77
   Textual analysis, 20–21
Legal research and writing courses,
   71–81
Letters of recommendation, 17, 32,
   117, 120, 122–123
Logos, 52–53, 54–55, 63, 89–90,
   106
Lucy v. Zehmer, 25–29, 158–165

                  M
Minorities in law school, 33
Mock trial. *See* Trial
Moot court, 71–81
   Oral argument
      Answering questions, 77–79
      Beginning the argument, 76–
         77
      Practicing for, 72, 74–75
      Preparing for, 71–75
      Tone, and use of, 80–81
      Using the right language, 79–
         80
      What to bring, 75–76
      What to expect, 75
Morse v. Frederick, 75

                  N
Networking, 139–140
Note-taking
   In class, 31–32

While reading. *See* Reading for
   class

                  O
Objections, making. *See* Trial
O'Connor, Sandra Day, 79–80
Office hours, visiting professors
   during, 120–121
On-campus interviews. *See* Inter-
   viewing for a job
Opening statements. *See* Trial
Oral advocacy/public speaking
   courses, 34, 43, 137
Oral argument. *See* Moot court
Organizations. *See* Student organi-
   zations
Outlining, 29–30

                  P
Pace, use of
   During job interviews, 131
   In presentations, 55, 64, 66–67
Pathos, 52–53, 54, 58, 63, 67, 88–
   89, 106
Pitch, use of
   During job interviews, 132
Plain meaning vs. purpose of the
   text, 21, 76, 102
PowerPoint, use of, 55, 56
Practice
   Delivering presentations, and,
      51, 57–58, 59, 60, 61, 63, 64,
      66, 67, 69
   Job interviews, and, 126, 131–
      133, 134–135, 137
   Leading a student organization,
      and, 113, 115
   Moot court oral argument, and,
      72, 74–75
   Socratic Method, and, 33–34, 36

Trial, and, 84, 86, 94, 95, 102
Workplace communication, and,
    141, 143, 144
Precedent, 19–20, 21, 22, 77
Presentations, 51–69
    Delivery of, 55, 59–67
        Body movement/language, 55,
            58, 60–62
        Eye contact, 65–66
        Gestures, and use of, 62–63
        Pace, and use of, 66–67
        Voice, and use of, 63–65
            Vocal warm-up exercises,
                65
    Engaging the audience, 61, 66
    Goals of, 52–53
    In a law firm, 51–52
    Overcoming fear of public speak-
        ing, and, 67–69
    Practicing for, 51, 57–58, 59, 60,
        61, 63, 64, 66, 67, 69
    Short notice delivery of, 58–59
    Transitions, and use of, 55, 56,
        61
    Visual aids, and use of, 55, 56,
        57, 59, 61, 63
    Writing a presentation, 53–57
        Engaging the audience, 56
        Introduction and conclusion,
            importance of, 55–56, 59
        Structuring presentations,
            54–55, 59
        Theme, use of, 53–54, 55,
            58–59
        Using clear language, and,
            56–57
Professors, interacting with, 17, 32,
    117–123
    Electronic communications, and,
        119–120

    In the classroom, 117–119
    Letters of recommendation, and,
        17, 32, 117, 120, 122–123
    Office hours, and, 120–121
    Working for, and, 121–122
Property law, 45–48
Public speaking
    Courses in, 34, 43, 137
    Fear of, 13, 33, 36, 37, 41–43,
        55, 59, 62, 67–69, 83–84

                    R
Reading for class
    Keeping up, 14–17, 37
    Reading cases, 17–30, 43–48
        Case-briefing, 25–29
        Highlighting, 25–26
        Holding/dicta distinction, 20
        Note-taking, 15, 16, 17, 24–
            25, 29
        Outlining, 29–30
        Paying attention to precedent,
            19–20
        Reading strategies, 15–16, 17–24
        Sources of law, 18–19
Refreshing witness recollection. See
    Trial
Regina v. Faulkner, 37–41, 166–170
Rehearsal/rehearsing. See Practice
Research assistant, working as, 121–
    122
Resume
    Being familiar with during job
        interviews, 126–127
Roberts, John, 73
Rogers, Will, 57
Roosevelt, Franklin Delano, 57
Rosenberger v. University of Virginia,
    79–80
Rule of law, 19

S

Sample Socratic questioning, 3–8, 37–41, 45–48

Self-consciousness, overcoming. *See* Socratic Method

Short notice presentations. *See* Presentations

Socrates, 8, 23

Socratic Method, *ix–x*, 3–11, 13–30, 31–49

    Final exams, and, 9, 14, 17

    Grades, and, *x*, 9, 14, 17

    Importance of, 3–11

    In-class strategies for, 31–49

        Not knowing the answer, 37–41

        Overcoming self-consciousness, 41–43

        Paying attention in class, 31–32

        Predicting common questions, 43–48

        Techniques for answering questions, 32–36, 49

    Interviewing for a job, and, 137

    Law practice, and, 9–10

    Origins and history of, 8–9

    Practicing for, 33–34, 36

    Preparing for, 13–30

        Case-briefing, 25–29

        Note-taking, 24–26

        Outlining, 29–30

    Sample class dialogue, 3–8, 37–41, 45–48

    Textual analysis, and, 21

    Thinking like a lawyer, and, 3–8

    Tone, and use of, 13, 35–36, 37, 49

    Use of hypotheticals, and, 6, 20, 22, 34, 44

Volunteering in class, and, 35, 42, 43

Speeches. *See* Presentations

Standard of review, 43

Stare decisis, 19

Starr, Kenneth, 73

Student organizations, 107–115

    Benefits of leading, 107–108

    How to lead a meeting of, 108–115

        Delegating tasks, 114

        Expecting the unexpected, 114–115

        Facilitating discussion, 111–112

        Preparing an agenda, 109

        Setting the right tone, 113

        Timekeeping, 109–110

    Practicing for, 113, 115

Studying, 14, 16–17, 128

Sullivan, Teresa, 142

Summer associate, working as. *See* Law firms

Supreme Court of the United States, 18, 19, 21, 73, 78, 79

Syllogism, use of, 22–23

T

Terms of art. *See* Jargon, use of

Textual analysis. *See* Legal reasoning

Thank you notes

    During callback interviews, 138

The Paper Chase, *ix*

The Rhetoric, 52

Theme, use of

    During job interviews, 126, 127, 128, 136, 137

    During trial, 88–89, 90, 91, 93, 105

    In presentations, 53–54, 55, 58–59

Theory of the case in trials. *See* Trial
Think, Breathe, and Answer technique, 34, 49
Thinking like a lawyer, 3–8
To Kill a Mockingbird, 83
Tone, use of
    During job interviews, 131, 137
    During presentations, 55
    During trial, 88, 95, 99
    In electronic communications, 120, 142, 143
    In oral argument, 80–81
    In student organizations, 113
    Socratic Method, and, 13, 35–36, 37, 49
Transitions, use of
    In presentations, 55, 56, 61
Trial, 83–106
    Arguing objections, and, 101–105
    Closing argument, and, 86, 89, 90, 91, 92, 105–106
    Cross-examination, and, 85, 86, 98–101
    Direct examination, and, 85, 86, 93–97
    Engaging the jury's attention, and, 89
    Entering exhibits into evidence, and, 89, 95, 96–97
    Ethos/credibility, and importance of, 86–88
    Impeaching a witness, and, 99–101
    Logic, and use of, 89–90
    Opening statement, and, 85, 89, 90–93
    Practicing for, 84, 86, 94, 95, 102
    Pre-trial activities
        Depositions, 93

    Discovery, 95, 143
    Refreshing witness recollection during, 96, 100
    Theory of the case, and, 88–89, 90, 91, 93, 105
    Tone, and use of, 88, 95, 99
    Visual aids, and use of, 87–88, 89, 105
    What it looks like/trial stages, 84–86
Trial advocacy/practice courses. *See* Trial

U
U.S. Constitution, 21, 78, 79–80
University of Pennsylvania Law School, 33
University of Virginia, 142
    School of Law, 13, 139

V
Visual aids, use of
    During trial, 87–88, 89, 105
    In presentations, 55, 56, 57, 59, 61, 63
Vocal warm-up exercises, 65
Voice, use of
    In presentations, 63–65
Vokes v. Arthur Murray, 3–8, 153–157
Volume, use of
    During job interviews, 131
    In presentations, 65
Volunteering in class, 35, 42, 43

W
Witnesses. *See* Trial
Women in law school, 33
Workplace communication, 141–149

Workplace communication, *cont'd*
   Asking questions, 144–145
   Electronic communication, 142–143
   In-person communication, 143–144
   Practicing for, 141, 143, 144
   Professional behavior, and, 145–149
Writing a presentation. *See* Presentations